MUSIC
AND
PHILOSOPHY

Gabriel Marcel

Music and Philosophy

Translated by
Stephen Maddux & Robert E. Wood

With an Introduction by
Robert E. Wood

MARQUETTE
UNIVERSITY
PRESS

Marquette Studies in Philosophy
No. 42
Andrew Tallon, Series Editor

Library of Congress Cataloging-in-Publication Data

Marcel, Gabriel, 1889-1973.
Music and philosophy / Gabriel Marcel ; translated by Stephen Maddux &
Robert E. Wood ; with an introduction by Robert E. Wood.
  p. cm. — (Marquette studies in philosophy ; no. 42)
Essays on music and its relation to his philosophy written by Gabriel Marcel in
French from various French journals.
Includes bibliographical references and index.
ISBN-13: 978-0-87462-665-0 (pbk. : alk. paper)
ISBN-10: 0-87462-665-X (pbk. : alk. paper)
  1. Music—Philosophy and aesthetics. I. Maddux, J. Stephen. II. Wood, Robert
E., 1934- III. Title. IV. Marquette studies in philosophy ; #42.
ML3800.M2413 2005
781'.1—dc22

2005025286

Cover photo of the Château Vaux-le-Vicomte, Maincy, France,
by Andrew J. Tallon, November, 2003.

Association of American
University Presses

MARQUETTE UNIVERSITY PRESS
MILWAUKEE

The Association of Jesuit University Presses

Epigraph

"Taken as a whole my work can be compared, I think, to a country like Greece, which comprises at the same time a continental part and islands. The continental part is my philosophical writing.... [T]he islands are my plays.... And...the element which unites the continent and the islands in my work is music. Music is truly the deepest level. In a certain way the priority belongs to music."

"Conversation with Paul Ricoeur"
Tragic Wisdom and Beyond

Table of Contents

List of Abbreviations

Life ....Music in My Life and Work"

Franck .... "The Musical Idea in César Franck"

Bergson .... "Bergson and Music"

Experience................. "Music Understood and Music Experienced"

Spirit ...."Music and the Reign of the Spirit"

Augustine................................ "Music According to St. Augustine"

Images................... "Response to the Inquiry into 'Musical Images'"

Marvelous ...."Music and the Marvelous"

Meditation .... "Meditation on Music"

Melody..."The Irruption of Melody"

Humanism .... "Humanism and Music"

Preface

Music played a central role in the thought of existentialist philosopher Gabriel Marcel (1889-1973). One of the most tantalizing claims he made in a set of conversations with Paul Ricoeur. Employing a geographic metaphor, he claimed that philosophy was the continent of his work while his plays formed the off-shore islands; but what was deepest was music as the water that conjoins the two.[1] One who wishes to understand how he thought of music will find that his philosophical writings contain only a few, quasi-aphoristic, though significantly penetrating things about the nature of music and its relation to his thought. Disappointingly, neither his short "An Essay in Autobiography" of 1947[2] nor his larger autobiography of 1971, *Awakenings*,[3] adds much to that beyond a few remarks. But the latter work makes reference to an article, "*La musique dans mon vie et mon oeuvre*," a lecture he delivered in Vienna in 1959, that turned out to be a significantly richer source.[4] And if one turns to his bibliography, one discovers that, as a music critic, Marcel published over 100 items on music—including "*Musique dans mon vie*".[5] None of them are available in English. Those of greater length and philosophical interest were gathered together, along with several shorter representative pieces, in the work entitled *L'esthétique musicale de Gabriel Marcel* that appeared in the *Presence de Gabriel Marcel* series.[6]

In order to enrich and deepen the appreciation of Marcel's thought in the English-speaking world by following up his understanding of the central role of music in his thought, but also to underscore the central importance of the aesthetic in human experience,[7] we have selected the main articles that appeared in that work for translation here. Marcel complained that (as of 1959) commentators had not paid significant attention to the close connection between music and philosophy. The present text should remedy that.

Our introduction attempts first to situate music in the whole of his work and to provide an overview of Marcel's observations that will follow in detail. It will begin with a brief exposition of the relation between the three areas of his lifework: his philosophic work, his dramatic work, and his musical work. We will explore the basic concepts of his thought and go on to recount how music played a role in his life. We will then attempt to gather together his remarks on the phenomenology of music and show how his observations on music and philosophy mutually illuminate both areas. We will conclude by locating his observations in relation to significant high-points in the history of philosophic reflection upon music. In so doing we wish to contribute to a re-situating of philosophy and a deepened understanding of music and its relation to comprehensive reflectiveness.

We have selected "*Musique et mon vie*" to lead off our translation of the major items of philosophical interest in *L'esthêtique*. After that as the chronologically latest, the others will be presented in chronological succession. *The List of Abbreviations* that follows this preface will be used parenthetically in our Introduction to refer to the articles gathered in this volume.

Institute of Philosophic Studies
University of Dallas

Notes

[1] *Tragic Wisdom and Beyond*, trans. S. Jolin and P. McCormick (Evanston: Northwestern University Press, 1973) (TWB), 231. The image of the sea representing the joining power of music was at least parallel to, if not influenced by, Wagner's *Art of the Future*. (Dahlhaus, *The Idea of Absolute Music* p.23)—hence-forth IAM.

[2] In *The Philosophy of Existentialism*, trans. M. Harari (New York: Citadel Press, 1956), 104-128 (henceforth PE).

[3] *Awakenings* (Milwaukee: Marquette University Press, 2002) (henceforth A).

[4] Ibid., 222. The lecture was published in 1965 as "Aperçus sur la musique dans ma vie et mon oeuvre" in *Livre de France*.

[5] Claude Troisfontaines, *De l'existence à la être: La philosophie de Gabriel Marcel*, 2 vols. (Louvain: Editions Nauwalaerts, 1968).

[6] Cahier 2-3, Paris: Aubier-Flammarion, 1980. Unless otherwise indicated, the notes to translated articles are to the notes provided by the editors of this work.

[7] For an achoring of that theme within the philosophical tradition, see my *Placing Aesthetics: Reflections on the Philosophical Tradition* (Athens: Ohio University Press, 1999).

Introduction

1.

Gabriel Marcel was considered the first twentieth century existentialist, i.e. a philosopher whose point of departure was reflection upon the nature of the individual human existent. However, he was not a philosopher of nihilistic despair or of defiant freedom such as characterized the popularized image of the existentialist in the mid-twentieth century, but placed himself in the company of Karl Jaspers, Martin Buber, and Martin Heidegger.[1] Like Buber, the Jewish existentialist who translated Hassidic Judaism into a philosophy accessible to believers and unbelievers alike, Marcel attempted the same translation for the presuppositions of his own Roman Catholic faith into a universally accessible philosophy.[2] But in addition to being a philosopher, Marcel was both a drama critic and a dramatist, whose dramatic output exceeded in bulk his philosophic works. Further, he was a music critic as well as a musician, who composed some thirty pieces for piano in the mode of Debussy and Ravel.

In looking back over his overall development, we already noted that he saw hidden connections between his philosophy, his dramatic works, and his interest in music. Love of theater and music implied "a passionate interest in individual beings and an irresistible attraction toward reality in its inexhaustible mystery."[3] But it was music, he said, that runs the deepest and that "commands the entire development of my thought."[4] As we shall see, he repeated that claim several times.

On the philosophic "continent," he worked through the concepts required to comprehend the human situation: concepts such as ontological weight, participation, feeling, inter-subjectivity, hope, and creative fidelity.[5] In clarifying them he employed distinctions between the lived body and the body-object, between problem and mystery, and, correspondingly, between primary and secondary reflection or between concentration and recollection.[6] He found the closest possible relation between these notions and his dramatic production that formed the "off-shore islands" of his work.[7] Philosophy requires both supplement and stimulus by reflection conducted within the element of life itself, in the full-bodied existence of characters in dialogical interaction that Marcel finds in drama. This removes his thought from abstraction and gives it an existential focus. In existential philosophy, he says, theater is the other side of the philosophy.[8] But both human action and human thought live in the deeper element of the surrounding mystery. Existence at its deepest is relation to the encompassing mystery of Being as a whole, the sense of which is a kind of feeling that guides the development of character as well as the categories of thought. In its most authentic form, relation to the mystery of being involves an all-pervasive sense of plenitude and cohesion. It was this feeling that gained expression in music, and hence about which Marcel could claim that it ran the deepest.[9] Music is the "sea" whose depths join the shores of philosophy and the islands of drama.

2.

Let us probe a bit further the categories of his philosophy. The central notion is *participation*.[10] Human life for Marcel is characterized by participation, found at the most rudimentary level in the relation between one's conscious life and one's body. In fact, he claimed that incarnate being was "the central datum of metaphysical reflection."[11] Feeling is the index, the sign, the manifestation of that participation.[12] When one sets about thinking of this, one is led to two abstract polarities: mind and body, which had been further abstracted by Descartes into thought and extension. Through empirical inquiry which attends away from the felt participation in one's own body to focus upon empirically available evidence—let us say regarding the physics and physiology of hearing—one is further led to the notion of a signal-sending-and-receiving system that culminates in the "interior" of awareness where the signal becomes heard sound. For Marcel the abstracted "interiority" of the experience is belied both by the lived sense of inhabitance and thus of a kind of identity with my body and, simultaneously, by one's participation through the experience of sound in what lies outside that putative interiority. Further, the body is not, like my car, something I *have*; it is something I *am*—though I am more than a body.[13] The split between inside and outside occurs through a first kind of reflection that abstracts from the fuller sense of participation in which we live.[14] Heard sound, reaching a certain level of perfection in music, takes us outside ourselves conceived of as occupying a private interiority.

But even this is an abstract rendering of an even more concrete aspect of participation: our sharing in the lives of significant others in and through our bodily based sensory experiences. The incarnation of the human spirit begins within the bosom of the family.[15] One lives in the overarching life of the family, of one's parents and siblings. One finds oneself, one is most fully one's self in their company. But they in turn are formed by the larger communities which condition and shape their peculiar coexistence. As in Aristotle and in Hegel, the concrete anchor of all forms of community lies in the family, though it is mediated by other wider relations of communal life.[16] It is in the family that Marcel locates the requirement of the basic dispositions of love, hope, and creative fidelity. It is the latter to which he gave special attention. Fidelity as he understands it is not simply endurance in coexisting with a given person; it requires creative work, the re-establishment again and again a sense of deepening presence.[17]

But participation does not stop here. By reason of the founding human structure of relation to the whole of what is via the notion of Being, there exists what Marcel calls an "ontological exigency," a demand of our nature to secure some sense of how we belong to that totality.[18] Thus all other modes of participation—in our body, in the surrounding environment, in our families and communities—are rafted upon a participation in the encompassing mystery of Being that for religious traditions is associated with the name 'God'. For thinkers like Heidegger and the Taoists, the mystery of Being is an impersonal encompassing; but with Marcel and in company with Buber and Levinas, the heart of the Mystery is a Thou, a confirming personal Presence we name 'God' or even dare to address as 'Father'.[19]

In thinking through the basic categories, the metaphor of seeing and the light enabling us to see runs through philosophy from the very beginning. In contrast with the predominantly visual metaphor, which Marcel also employs, he appeals primarily to an aural metaphor in describing his thought, namely the metaphor of music. He even, paradoxically, fuses the two when speaking of music as "the saving light" (Life 52). But, as we shall see, music is more than a metaphor;

it is rather the ground and, in a sense, the substance of his thought, its deepest aspect, its generating source.

> I am not a spectator who is looking for a world of structures suscep-
> tible of being viewed clearly and distinctly, but rather...I listen to the
> voices and appeals comprising that symphony of Being—which is
> for me, in the final analysis, a supra-rational unity beyond images,
> words, and concepts.[20]

The spectator's vision allows us to stand at a distance and view an object passive to our gaze; listening allows the initiative to be taken by the other which makes claims upon us. Vision gives us the model for what Marcel calls, alternatively employing the Greek and Latin derivatives, *problem* and *object*, both imaging what has been cast (*blema* and *jectum*) before (*pro* and *ob*) an observer.[21] Thus one can consider a mechanical problem which stands before one's visual eye or a math-ematical problem which stands before one's mental eye. One becomes a detached spectator, setting the object or problem upon which we concentrate intellectually at a distance. Contrasted with object and problem, there are *presence* and *mystery*, characterized as *participa-tory*. Presence is capable of deepening and is correlated with concern. What is a living presence for me is something in which I participate, something without which I cannot properly conceive myself. "Over there" is simultaneously "in here." Such participatory encroachment upon what could, only under certain aspects, be objectified Marcel terms *mystery*.[22] One is unable to separate oneself from such partici-pation in order to secure an objective mastery. Thus one's own body is a mystery; one's sensory awareness of what lies outside oneself is a mystery; one's relation to one's family, beloved, friends is a mystery; and the way in which all of this is horizoned by a sense of the totality is the final *ontological mystery*. For all this, as in relation to one's own body, feeling is the sign, the index of participation. The deeper our participation, the more it tends to rise to the level of feeling. Feeling, participation, presence, and mystery go together. Indeed, Marcel has said that "my thinking takes its departure above all from feeling, from reflection on feeling and on its implications."[23]

One begins reflection by detachment from the lived patterns of participation and by concentration upon the objectification of certain aspects of experience. This is what Marcel calls "first reflection." As objectification proceeds in the scientific-technological mode and advances until it becomes *the* mode of thought, we enter into what Marcel calls "the broken world": mind broken off from body, sensation from its objects, aspects of thought and action from other aspects and from each other.[24] More significantly, as this pattern of thought becomes dominant, people are broken off from one another and humankind from the divine. Manipulation replaces participation and the holy disappears. Human beings become cogs in a machine. Music for Marcel gives testimony to that which protests against this condition (Life 66).

But there is another mode of reflection which Marcel calls "second reflection" or *recollection* as a re-collection of our self scattered into various functions.[25] Recollection secures a kind of "inward grip" upon oneself as a whole. He claims that this "inward grip" was provided for him particularly by the practice of improvisation on the piano (Melody 101; Spirit 113-4). To secure it is to experience a particular sort of attunement, a feeling which is better described as a listening rather than as a seeing. At the same time, this grip, paradoxically, is a letting go of the grasping mode, a letting of oneself be claimed by that to which one listens. It is all the more required in the modern world when the sense, the feeling of participation has tended to evaporate. It is here that Marcel joins Heidegger in the latter's talk about "the forgottenness of Being" as the element in which humans live, whose language is the "house of Being."[26] Under the dominance of objectification and the consideration of everything as at hand for our projects, the world ceases being our home. In contrast, Marcel described his own thought as "the metaphysics of at home."[27]

Let us turn to a consideration of the way music came to be for him "the saving light" that showed the way for philosophic reflection and that eventually led to his religious conversion.

3.

...it is music and music alone that has caused me to discover the saving light. It is music that has opened the road to Truth for me, towards which I have not ceased striving, this Truth beyond all the partial truths that science demonstrates and expounds, the Truth

that illumines the work of the greatest composers like Bach or
Mozart. (Life 53)

A musical phrase by Bach or Beethoven...seemed invested with a
supreme authority which did not allow of any explanation. One was
beyond knowledge and yet it was as if one breathed a certainty which
went infinitely beyond the limits of a simple, individual emotion
deriving from a particular temperament or sensitivity. The greatest
musical works seemed to invoke directly a certain communion.[28]

Through a phrase from Brahms...I have suddenly come to see that
there is a universality which is not of the conceptual order; that is
the key to the idea of music. But how hard it is to understand. The
idea can only be the fruit of a kind of spiritual gestation.[29]

...it is music, and music almost exclusively, which has been for me
an unshakable testimony of a deeper reality in which it seemed to
me that everything fragmentary and unfulfilled on the sensory level
would find fulfillment.[30]

* * *

In looking back over his life, Marcel remarked that "...music has not
only played a great role, it has been one of the original components of
my very being...." (Life 42), "the saving light" as the milieu and deep
source of his philosophic thought and dramatic production.[31]

Marcel's father was passionately devoted to music but could not find
the categories that allowed him to accept religion. Music became for
young Gabriel, as it had been for his father, a kind of surrogate for
religion. But for Marcel, such surrogate status did not make it inauthentic, for he later reflected that music at its deepest turns into prayer
(Franck 82; Spirit 114). Immersion in music is a kind of response to
a call, an openness to being seized and simultaneously coming into
possession of oneself (Images 125). It was, indeed, through music that
Marcel himself came to religious faith.

A graphologist remarked to him that his handwriting indicated
that he escaped from depression through contact with nature and
with music (Life 44). Marcel was astonished at how accurate that
was. But the conjunction was not accidental. He testified that "I

have felt the power of incantation since my childhood in music as in certain landscapes."[32] This was especially awakened during his walks as a boy in the forests surrounding Stockholm when his father was cultural ambassador to Sweden. He found there "a natural symphony of water, stones, pines and birches" (Life 44). This attracted him to the music of Grieg and especially Schumann. Later he spoke of his love of American wilderness[33] and of the harmony of art and nature he found in Japan.[34] He recognized in Debussy in particular a composer "penetrated by the mysterious power of nature" (Humanism 142), as seen especially in *Pelléas et Mélisande* with the music of the forest, the sea, the garden, and sunlight (Meditation 130). He also remarked on the ardent love for sensory beauty—whether of nature or of art—that endured throughout his life.[35] Sensory beauty was invested from the beginning with an encompassing halo of enchantment that gave him an enduring sense of "the mystery of being."

He learned to play the piano, studied composition and, as we noted, throughout his life recovered his grip on himself through improvisation (Spirit 113-4; Melody 137-8). He was attracted to poetry of the most musical sort, and later composed music for poems by authors such as the Frenchmen Baudlaire, Lamartine, and Valery, and the Germans Rilke, Hölderlin and Hoffmannsthal. He even thought at one time that he would become a composer and subsequently conjectured that he could have done so with some success (Melody 138; Life 46, 52). Later in 1946-7 his wife Jacqueline—whom he married "under the musical sign of Bach's *Concerto for Two Violins*"[36]—transcribed thirty of his improvisations into musical notation, some renditions of which are now available in CD form.[37] He claimed that these melodies, more than his philosophical works, clearly delineate the direction of his thought.[38]

At sixteen he discovered philosophy in a kind of conversion experience. For him it was a search for God and immortality (Life 47). The link with music was close: he says, "in conditions that can only remain mysterious, music has always been for me, in the course of this hectic philosophical quest I have pursued, a permanent guarantee of that reality that I was attempting to reach by the arid paths of pure reflection" (Life 65). Music, he said, gave him "a blind intuition," "a mysterious assurance," "a kind of communion" and a sense of plenitude and cohesion that led him to reflect upon being (Life 46).[39] And in thinking about being, rather than beginning with the categories of science or the categories involved in thinking about the external world, Marcel began with what he claimed was revealed through music.

To speak of what music delivers as a "blind intuition" is paradoxical: a non-seeing sight! 'Intuition' involves immediate givenness, but is usually linked with visual presentation that masters what is given. To speak of it as "blind" is to cancel the visual dominance and yet retain the immediacy. The "mysterious assurance" involved an "unshakable testimony of a deeper reality in which...everything fragmentary and unfulfilled at the sensory level would find fulfillment."[40] Attunement to the symphony, the correspondences, the togetherness of all things, provides a sense of cohesion and plenitude, a guiding sense that things fit together, that emptiness of meaning does not have the last word.[41]

Following a path of reflection on being brought about by musical experience, Marcel at age forty was received into the Catholic Church. As he said, it was Bach infinitely more than Pascal, a musician more than a thinker, that started him on the road to this conversion (Life 41). Music at its depth became prayer and led him to the categories that his father lacked for recognizing what stirred in the depth of his musical experience. The focal notion was the notion of being to which he referred as the essential mystery.

Reflection on being is the guiding thread through the history of philosophy. Going back to Parmenides and enduring through Hegel and Heidegger, the identity of thought and being is a constant. The notion of being furnishes the "light" within which what appears to us can appear in its way of appearing to human beings. Initially empty, the notion of being in us aims at the Whole, for outside being is nothing, and all that is is contained within its scope. The notion of being grounds our distinctive humanness: pointing us to the Whole, it pries us loose from all determinants, calls for the filling of the empty space of meaning between the ever-present, ever-flowing Now of sensory encounters and the encompassing Whole, and condemns us to choose our way according to our always limited understanding of our place in the whole scheme of things.

One might say that for Marcel there is a double identity of thought and being: of thought with one's own being and of thought with encompassing being. Rather than thought about an object or subject, thinking about being is thinking about that which encompasses subject and object, and yet it is grounded in the peculiarity of the human subject who is referred, beyond its own subjectivity, to being as a whole. Much turns upon the kind of identity thought has with being in oneself and as the Whole. The notion of being includes the whole of oneself and not simply one's "intellect," although reference to being as the encompassing Whole founds intellect as the ability to apprehend the truth of various regions within that Whole. For Marcel what is crucial is how one's own wholeness is related to the encompassing. For him, the "light of Being" is not simply intellectual reference but concrete dwelling, participating in the mystery of encompassment. Hence the identity of thought and being is not "knowledge" but a certain "sense" given in and by music (Meditation 133).

In a phrase from Brahms he said he discovered a universality not of the conceptual order that is the key to the idea of music. The universal is "the element in which the mind finds its substance and takes flight" (Spirit 105). Science and philosophy on the one hand and the arts on the other aim at the universal. But in music, as in art in general, the universality is found in the concrete singular (Spirit 112). Images and words can be developed into art forms beyond concepts, such as painting and poetry; but the distance of the image from the observer and the proximity to the conceptual in the poetic word distinguish these art forms from music. And yet, Marcel says, with Walter Pater, that all art seeks the status of music as aesthetic form evoking a felt sense of participation.[42] But some artists are more musical than others: Watteau and Rembrandt are more so than Boucher or Frans Hals (Spirit 106). And Marcel noted the musical character of his own dramatic works. Of course, the art form that is most proximate to music is poetry for which the sound is essential to the meaning conveyed in words. This is what led Marcel to his own earliest compositions, providing musical accompaniment to his favorite poems. However, he noted that not all poems equally lend themselves to such a move (Melody 138). In an image parallel to a favorite of John Dewey's, apart from images, words, and concepts, yet not necessarily without them, music expresses and articulates the milieu in which they swim.[43]

If philosophy seeks the truth of being, for Marcel, "music, and music alone, tells the truth" (Life 56, where Marcel quotes from his play, *Quartet in F Sharp*). Here he distinguishes between Truth and truths (Life 48-9). Music gives utterance to the "light of Truth" as the encompassing within which all partial truths appear. And that Truth, he said, is identical with a person. This expression he leaves in ambiguity. It might sound like God is this Truth. That would follow if, as he said, music in its depths shades off into prayer, so that our participation in the mystery of Being shades off into encounter with God. But more proximately, the person identical with the Truth, I think, is the self whose whole being, directed beyond its privacy to the Whole, "illuminates" the philosophic search. Remember, for Marcel music was "one of the original components of my very being" (Life 42). What stirs in the deepest musical experience is not some fleeting private feeling; it is the whole of oneself as directed to the encompassing mystery.

Music, he tells us, was not so much the object of reflection as it was the wellspring of thought, the *pensée pensante*, thought think-ing, rather than the *pensée pensée,* thought thought about. Music, in a sense, is identical with the subject-pole that guides thought about the object-pole but which, paradoxically, refers beyond itself and its possible objects to that which encompasses both the self and its ob-jects. The notion of communion fits here as underscoring the idea of participation. Here one does not stand at a distance viewing an object; one communes with it as one does with a person. It is not something external but something identical with one's own being, without which one is not oneself.

In his "Essay in Autobiography," he links his sense of the supra-sensuous with the discovery of Schopenhauer's theory of music.[44] For Schopenhauer, the cosmos is the expression of an underlying Will which forms the phenomenal world through Platonic Ideas but which gains immediate expression through music. This places conceptual work in second place beneath the sense of the Whole cultivated by music.[45] Schopenhauer's view of music turned Marcel away from an optical imagining of the supra-sensuous such as he thought dogged the notion of Platonic archetypes (Life 53). It was this sense of the Whole beyond concepts that also turned him away from beginning with concepts derived from observing the external world and led him to formulate our more primordial relation to the encompassing Whole. Needless to say, the sense of cohesion and plenitude anticipated in music was not, for Marcel, a mask for the underlying self-contradiction of the cosmic Will in the pessimism of Schopenhauer.

Music testifies to the in-principle inadequacy of all our attempts at conceptual comprehension of the totality of being to which we are referred in our distinctive humanness. It is this reference which grounds science, philosophy, and religion. Music articulates the totality in a participative mode open to all humankind. By reason of the fundamental orientation of human existence to the encompassing mystery of Being, that space of meaning opened up in music is something more than the togetherness of composer, performer and audience. It is not simply solidarity with other humans that is at issue. It is a sense of plenitude and consistency with regard to reality as a whole. The assurance that existence transcends objectification was given by music, "a mysterious and unshakable testimony" invoking a communion, a type of universality in confrontation with the individual musical object.[46]

As he linked his philosophic interest to music, so Marcel linked his interest in music to his dramatic work: "Music offered me an irrefutable example of the kind of supra-rational unity which I believed to be the essential function of drama to establish and to promote."[47] His theater he described as "musical in its very essence." (Life 53) In his account of music in his life and work, he ends with rather long excerpts from his plays *Quartet in F Sharp, The Dart*, and *My Time Is Not Yours* (Life 55-69) where music is not simply the generative source, but becomes an explicit theme. The off-shore islands of drama arose out of the deep waters of musical experience. His larger autobiography ends by repeating the claim that his philosophical efforts translated within the language of thought and his dramatic effort into the language of dialogue the triumphant assurance provided by Beethoven and Schubert.[48]

4.

Marcel's reflections on music are based upon careful phenomenological description that attempts to lay out the essential features of musical reality. It is in phenomenology, he said, "and in that alone that it is possible today to find solid ground for a philosophy of musical experience" (Augustine 121-2). There is a sense in which this approach also governs his approach to his dramatic works: "The point here is not, . . . in my . . . plays, to demonstrate or to refute but only to show" (Life 56).

A phenomenology of music would distinguish and relate composer, performer, work, and hearer, although musical experience involves the conjoining of them all. Our exposition will thus necessarily involve the trespass of one factor upon the others. But we will proceed by making one or the other sequentially focal. We begin with the work.

The score is clearly not the musical work any more than the recipe is the cake (Experience 97). Based upon the score, the performer produces the work as the deliberate articulation of sound. The deliberateness places it in kinship with language as a transformation of sound into the carrier of meaning; that makes it supra-sensuous. But in music, sound is not, as in ordinary conversation, subsidiary to the meaning communicated; it is focal, even when it accompanies lyrics. As in all art, the sensuous is not mere carrier of meaning; it is itself part of the meaning. Every art is "an expression radiating from the mystery of incarnation" and "a potency of incarnation," that is, the possibility of giving flesh to meaning (Spirit 103-4). As we will see, such enfleshing is not simply sensory presence; it is the presence of human vitality, spiritually incarnate experience. But that means that the work is inseparable from its entry into the life of its audience.

However, in the case of the plastic arts, the distance of the image from the observer and, in the case of linguistic arts, the proximity to the conceptual in the word distinguish these art forms from music. Contrary to the case of language, as we have noted, for Marcel the meaning in music is not "rational"; it is "supra-rational." That sets it beyond concepts. That is why he claimed that his philosophy, fed by music, is not so much rooted in reflection upon language as upon the incarnate condition revealed in sensuousness.[49]

We could continue to speak of music in a most external way as the production of vibrations that, in turn, produce sound in relation to a hearer. Like every other sensory power, the capacity to perceive sound sets up a relation that would not be there without the sensor

and the sensed. The sensory features of things are relations of physical things to consciousness (Spirit 103). Sensing, however, does not
lock us into our privacy; it brings us out into a world of things other
than ourselves.

Now music is not just sound, it is diachronic sound, sound organized over time, as it is also synchronic sound, the contemporaneous
production of harmonic relations. A musical piece is form embedded
in a system of sounds (Experience 98). Each musical sound stands in
a relation to other sounds that modify it simultaneously and successively (Experience 99; Augustine 117). All of that could be transcribed
mathematically; but all that would still be a very external relation to
musical reality (Spirit 104).

Sound passes away as it is generated, and one sound succeeds another
only to disappear, until the whole series is completed in execution.
But then it is irrevocably gone. As Marcel noted, music expresses "the
tragic tension implicit in the struggle against time" (Augustine 118).
Musical reality as such exists only in the memory of the hearer who
retains as much as possible the whole sequence when listening (Bergson
87). The work then exists as a "non-spatial figure" that transcends the
duration in which it is revealed (Bergson 89). Boris de Schloezer would
maintain that the piece is held in the immobile and silent judgment
that grasps the unity of what is retained (Augustine 118).

But over and above impression, memory, and recognition in judgment, harmonic relations have affective effects that Marcel variously
describes as "magical" or "incantatory" or "marvelous" or "enchanted"
or "haunted". Here is where the ways begin to part. Marcel takes on de
Schloezer who, having located authentic musical experience in intellectual recognition, rejects "the magical" or "the marvelous" as aspects
of merely emotional appeal (Experience 101). But there is a radical
distinction between intellectual recognition and felt appreciation. It
is the distinction between problem and mystery translated into the
musical sphere. There is the danger of missing the lyricism that vitalizes the formal (Experience 100). A person may have an acute power
of intellectual recognition without the music "speaking" to him or
her. Musical "speech" is the power of enchantment, of incantation, of
"magic". The primitive musician has a direct relation to this feature
(Marvelous 128). The magical is "the very flesh of music" as it is,

indeed, he says enigmatically, the human soul itself (Marvelous 127). The mathematical and intellectual features of music are, as it were, the skeleton; it is the lyrical, the magical that gives music its living body as it comes to inhabit the hearer. Music thus operates in the zone where the soul as animating principle "haunts" the body.

As we noted, from the early years of his life Marcel experienced the power of incantation in the landscape and in music simultaneously, each calling out to the other. In his longer autobiography, he spoke of the "incantatory force" of some of Wagner's musical phrases and of Debussy and Fauré as conjurers (Bergson 112). Inspired work, he said, is "inhabited" (Spirit 112). "If it is not charm and magic, music is nothing but mathematics or scholasticism." (Marvelous 128) The incantatory force produces a "fairy space" that is not something we intellectually recognize; it is something we deeply feel. Indeed, feeling is the very essence of music.

In much of the philosophic tradition feeling was considered sub-rational, arising by reason of spirit's incarnate condition, its link with the body and thus with what was regarded as the lowly level of matter.[50] As we noted, the incarnate character of human being, the main them of Marcel's work, brings the human spirit out of its tendency toward solipsism and into community with others.[51] Feeling is the index of that participation. Though there are sub-rational feelings, like the desire for food, feeling can also be supra-rational. Marcel's thought is based upon a type of feeling that brings to awareness our belonging to the Whole, beyond the limited here-and-now manifest in bodily-based sensations and the diversity of culturally grounded activities. In playing Brahms he spoke of "this feeling of being entered, of being absolutely safe—and also of being enfolded."[52] Such a feeling sets the direction for conceptual development but also inserts abstract conceptualization back into the concrete totality.

Let us return to the notion that music produces "a fairy space." In such space, he says, "near and far pass into one another." (Marvelous 128) There seem to be two aspects here that are displayed in our relation to whatever we intensely love: on the one hand, physical distance is overcome in personal proximity and, on the other hand, even in physical proximity a certain encompassing distance from everything else occurs. In contrast, our ordinary relations are "a dialogue between

absences" (Spirit 112). But there is another feature: the nearness of
the far, the coming to presence of what encompasses all. When a being takes us out of the everyday, out of ourselves, one's life as a whole
is rearranged, magnetized by the intensity of a new presence. One's
heart is addressed in a transformative way, so that such presence haunts
our lives wherever we might go or whatever we might do. This "fairy
space" is the space of presence, of nearness and distance at once.
Musical mystery, Marcel claimed, is the mystery of presence (Spirit
112) that gives rise to "intimacy" (Images 126; Melody 138). Music
is, in another of his enigmatic phrases, the emergence of a form that is
"wedded, recreated from within" (Spirit 113). The "wedding" points
to the intimacy of musical presence in which the configuration of the
sensuous is transferred from the external space of sound production into
the interiority of the hearer in such a way as to bring the hearer out of
himself or herself and into relation with the encompassing Whole. It
is as Heidegger noticed: in a great work of art so much "world space"
is created that even the ordinary appears extraordinary.[53]

The work that enters into form and transforms the hearer has a
peculiar identity in the differences of its performances. Like Roman
Ingarden, Marcel distinguishes the musical work and the musical performance.[54] Though in a sense fixed in the score, the work is capable
of differing incarnations in sound. The deeper the work the more
the possible interpretations. While a score can determine exactly the
harmonic or dissonant relations between tones, it can only describe
vaguely the dynamic features, fast or slow, loud or soft, in relation to
the piece experienced as a whole. A performer must learn to indwell
in the work, to feel its wholeness and to balance the differing dynamic
qualities in their relation to the whole work. Even the composer
might interpret these features differently in different performances
(Spirit 108).[55]

At the origin of the enchanting, the magical, the incantatory, there is
the musician's soul which is "a haunted soul." (Augustine 120). What
haunts him or her is what Marcel calls "the musical idea" as something
that the composer finds rather than invents (Spirit 109): it confronts
him like a person, a thou who calls for a response (Franck 72). There
is a double response here: whatever one encounters, the musical idea,
he says, is an answer or an affirmation that requires re-creation (Spirit

109). This peculiar claim requires a prior search through which the composer encounters the musical idea as a response to that search. But, like a person, the musical idea in turn requires the response of creation in fidelity to what is presented in it.

The musical idea is not a concept; it is a peculiar feeling, a certain emotion, that may at first be like "an aural nebula" (Spirit 109). The disposition involves the ability to translate feeling into musical form. But, Marcel claims, music dos not simply *express* feeling; he stoutly claims that it *is* feeling itself freed from its psychosomatic matrix and clarified by becoming a structure in and above time (Life 49). Such translation involves a working through the emotion to reach a trans-conceptual universality that "distills essences" (Spirit 104). Taking on musical form, the differing feelings involved are like concepts: they illuminate their instances; they convey insight into what holds for all instances. The composer thereby becomes spokesperson for an infinity of souls (Spirit 111) . Marcel is close here to Susanne Langer who held that art creates symbolic forms expressive of an understanding of the life of feeling incapable of translation into any other medium.[56]

Marcel said that the musical idea is "the dynamic equivalent of a disposition" (Franck 77). He goes on to say that it has a certain "direction". Some musical ideas come to down to us from above. Some of Cesar Franck's music he sees as parallel to the best of Bach: it has the ability to express the divine solicitude that descends upon us. Beethoven's Fifth, on the other hand, is directed toward us in an overpowering manner bent upon taming us. And some of Schumann embodies the longing, the outward and upward movement of the human heart.

But what is involved is not only the presentation of the essence of this or that type of feeling; the composer presents "an individualized *world* of primordial experience" (Meditation 130), a world sharable in principle by all (Spirit 105). He or she has a way of comprehending the one and only reality, both seizing and being embraced beyond isolated subjectivity (Images 125). Nonetheless, the composer operates out of the depth of subjectivity as his or her modulation of relation to the Whole that belongs in principle to all humans.

What is "primordial experience"? Perhaps the language of feeling here is insufficient, since for Marcel primordial experience takes place beyond the contrast of faculties that here reveals the "crude insufficiency" of our usual contrasts (Meditation 130). Music speaks in a holistic way; it provides an experience that transcends the division of faculties. Here Marcel seems close to Maritain's observations on poetry that proceeds from "the single root of the soul's powers."[57] Marcel speaks of music as involving "a pure erotic" (Augustine 120) revealing the world of primordial experience that is neither intellectual nor simply emotional (Meditation 93). It is basically the world of childlike wonder and enchantment that is lost through routine (Meditation 129-30). This is an interesting gloss on the biblical "Unless you become as little children...."[58]

There is another dimension of musical creation: that of entering into a musical tradition that provides the genres within which a composer operates. The composer constructs within the context of the rules defining the genre or creates rules for a new genre within which he and others can work. Marcel cites with approval Valéry's observation on "the stimulating and propulsive character of restraints." (Melody 138) Like the rules of a game, the rules of a genre allow one to focus and hone one's powers to a perfection not available in random action.

Regarding the performer Marcel remarks on his own improvisation where "a barrier was broken through and I then had the feeling of gaining entrance into myself and at the same time of evolving, with an ease that astonished me, inside an unknown world in which the possibilities of discovery were seemingly inexhaustible" (Life 51). Here, however, he is composing as he performs. But in the case of performing from a score, as we already noted, there is a difference between the work and the performance, since the same work can be given diverse interpretations. The incarnation of the work is at the mercy of the performer: he or she can do more or less justice to it or can massacre it. Each time a performer plays a given piece it has as it were to be re-created anew. The quality of the performance depends upon the current state of the performer as well as upon the level of technical ability (Experience 97). In sight reading, Marcel notes "the quasi-simultaneity of the act by which this silent music constitutes itself in the soul itself and the act by which it incarnates itself and takes on material form in sound" (Augustine 118). The more superficial the work, the more performance tends towards stereotypical identity;

the deeper the work, the more creative the interpretations possible (Spirit 100-8). However, what Marcel calls the "musical object" depends upon both performer and hearer (Spirit 107). (Of course, the performer is also a hearer.)

As the origin of music lies in feeling awakened in the composer and reawakened in the performer, hearing it by the audience culminates in feeling (Humanism 141). It frees in the hearer the feeling that was at the origin of the piece. The heard melody remains more living, having taken on body (Augustine 118). Here the "body" is the magic, the lyricism.

One must be careful to distinguish types of musical feeling. There is the merely pleasant which pleases only in an instant and to which the hearer remains primarily passive (Franck 71). This corresponds to the work that can be repeated stereotypically because it has no depth. In its deeper reaches, the feeling involved in music involves a re-creation by the hearer. For Marcel, there is a hierarchy of persons parallel to the hierarchy of works: the deeper the work the more one has to draw upon one's own depths in real listening (Spirit, 114).

Marcel speaks of the deepest works as having "existence," "power of affirmation," and "authority". The use of the term 'existence' here is idiosyncratic. It is parallel to Heidegger's claim that great works of art are works that *are,* "preserved" in their working by those who allow themselves to be taken into their revealing power rather than in their merely empirical existence as works that *were.*[59] "Power of affirmation" refers to the ability of such works to renew themselves, but also to reveal themselves only little by little (Franck 71). Merely pleasant works show themselves immediately. Those that have "power of affirmation" show themselves only after repeated hearings, and the greatest reveal themselves in ways virtually inexhaustible. This is true both in listening and in performing.

Music that has this power of affirmation has authority over us and transforms us (Franck 72-3) . "The real, the living idea is the one that, when it has completed its work, does not leave us as it found us" (Franck 73). Such music is capable of effecting the restoration of man to himself (Spirit 114). Like a person, in revealing itself it reveals ourselves to ourselves and has the kind of authority that can lead, beyond authority, to fellowship (Franck 73). A great musical work is a commanding presence that can become something like a friend.

If music brings us into the mystery of presence, such presence has an essential relation to both the past and the future. Music sets us meaningfully in time. First of all, music for Marcel arises out of a global feeling which summarizes one's past.[60] Secondly, it grounds our hope in the future since it testifies that reality is not meaningless but ultimately has cohesion and plenitude. And in summarizing the past and grounding the future at the level of global feeling, it establishes a deepened present.

For Marcel music and memory are intimately linked (Spirit 114). He speaks of the past experienced in music as typically "under-utilized" in ordinary life (Bergson 58). It involves a "re-memoration of myself" without referring explicitly to past events, perhaps because, as he claims, it involves a global rather than a specific feeling. It is helpful to think here of the notion of the heart as the reservoir of one's past in regard to what has personal significance. The past endures globally at the level of the heart where everything that we have experienced is filtered down to that which has come to have meaning for us as individuals. The heart has as its correlate charged presences, magnetic attractors that automatically solicit our attention, in whose direction we are spontaneously inclined to move. Music addresses the heart—music and love, as Marcel says. A new piece, he claims, can be "recognized" as corresponding to this under-utilized past. It is as if one knew it beforehand precisely because it corresponds to the depth of one's past. Musical feeling presents itself as object of a fulfilled expectation answering to a hitherto hidden emptiness (Bergson 90).

The linkage of music with one's past has a special relation for Marcel to those who have been meaningfully involved in one's life (Life 55, 65): music restores "through the sacrament of sound all those who have shared my life" (Melody 137). But music only brings to presence what hovers in the background of all our experience. Marcel regarded as one of the most significant lines in all his plays a remark from *le Dard*: "If there were only the living...I think the earth would be completely uninhabitable." In his "metaphysics of at-home," inhabitance has to do with how we are inserted in time with others, how those who have passed and those who are to come enter into the fabric of our sense of the present. Here he joins the various cultural traditions in which familial piety, piety for the ancestors and committment to familial and communal continuance are continuous with piety towards the Ground of all.

In his *Quartet in F Sharp* one of the characters asks: "Isn't music like the immortality of everything we think is dead but in fact lives on?" (Life 55) Even more mysterious, he says, than bearing the sense of truth, music bears witness to victory over death (Life 48-9). These last two comments, read in isolation from their context, might be considered to refer to the continuing performance of works by those long dead. Subjectively mortal, the composers stand immortal in their works. But that is not what he means—or at least not primarily. In his comments on his improvisation, he remarks:

> what is here in question is . . . a sublimation that tends to convert into essences the beings that it has been given to me either to cherish or simply to envelop with a glance of momentary longing. . . It is as if, in musical improvisation, this longing—a longing to which so often the mutual knowing of erotic love (*co-naissance erotique*) can contribute only the most precarious and the most fallacious satisfactions—found a marvelous though fleeting answer to a prayer (Melody 101).

Such citations show that for Marcel the borders of a personality are extended into everything he/she cares for.[61] But music's special role is to attain to a renewed presence, a communion, even with those who affected one but casually, within a sense awakened by music of the encompassing Whole.

In spite of all that rings true to me in what Marcel says about music, I must admit that when I read such claims about relation to the dead that had directly affected his life, I draw a blank. Is this anything more than testimony to the peculiar associations he had in his experience of music? Does it have the universality of a whole set of his other claims?

But even apart from its relation to the endurance of those with whom one is identified, for Marcel music is "a pledge of eternity" (Spirit 114). He sees the kind of certitude this involves to be of a piece with the kind of belief that is far from the arrogant self-assurance of "the righteous." "The true believer has a share in eternity; he knows it; he judges all things from the point of view of eternity" (Franck 78)—though such assurance is linked to a humility and thankful-ness far removed from the arrogance of the righteous. The musical idea is the object of a belief rooted in a peculiar sort of experience; it is communication with another order of being. This is the depth dimension in which the musical idea seems to "come from afar" in order to introduce us to "a relaxation of effort coming from above." (Bergson 93) The last odd phrase suggests that what is given in such musical experience is experienced as a release from ourselves by giving us access to the hidden mystery that surrounds the everyday and that corresponds to our own hidden depths. Marcel speaks in this regard of a "musical mysticism" (Bergson, 94) and of an authentic spiritual-ity found in the best works of Bach, Mozart, Beethoven, Schumann, Brahms, and Fauré (Experience 102).

All this is adjunct to the claim that fellowship with the musical idea is linked to the establishment, through the sensuous and simultaneous supra-sensuous character of music, of an in-principle universal inter-subjectivity beyond Eris, beyond the contentiousness of argument that afflicts the philosophic and religious communities. As Marcel said, "Music appears as the sensuous, and at the same time supra-sensuous, expression of that inter-subjectivity which opens philosophic reflection to the discovery of the concrete *thou* and *us*."[62] Music gives access to the heart of a foreign culture (Spirit 105) because music transcends boundaries within a culture and beyond any given culture. As testimony to this power of music, the opening sessions of the United Nations begin with Beethoven's rendition of Schiller's "Ode to Joy."

The thou and the we are joined in their deepened relation to being as a whole and can lead to a kind of natural mysticism that puts an end to unavailability (Bergson 94). Such "mysticism" is not simply a momentary high that might be provided by drugs or sex or even run-ning, for these do not bring us out of our privacy and closure. They rather fortify us in it. The mysticism to which Marcel refers baths our whole life, brings us out of ourselves, and makes us open for what might address us in our lives.[63]

Here he makes explicit reference to Heidegger's notion of the Open and Rilke's notion interior cosmic space (Meditation 135). Heidegger discusses the two together.[64] The Open is the element in which humans live, like fish live in water. As with Marcel's view of the function of music, it is a space beyond conceptualization that undercuts and grounds distinctions between active and passive, intellect and feeling, intelligible and sensible, from me and from elsewhere, far and near (Meditation 135). The Open is "the ground of metaphysics" as relation to the hidden out of which the manifest arises. In Rilke as in Heidegger it relates to the inner space of the heart as the unitary ground of the differing capacities of the human individual. For Marcel music establishes community by articulating this inner space.

At the same time as Marcel underscores our belonging to community, he also describes himself as "a sower of silence" and "a sower of solitude."[65] This parallels Max Picard's observations on silence and music: great music arises out of silence and sets us back into silence.[66] Such solitude and such silence, far from separating us from others, are rather the bases for communion with them. Silence and speech as well as solitude and community are not exclusive opposites so much as they are mutual requirements of authentic human existence. Speech which does not carry with it a sense of silence tends towards chatter; community that is not counterbalanced by a love for solitude, and solitude which is not significantly more than a running away from other people are both flights from reality. It would not seem amiss to read Marcel's view of music in a similar vein. Great music arises out of silence and sets us back into silence; it arises out of the composer's silence and establishes the community of listeners who are taken outside their privacy into a communal space of trans-rational meaning. A silence of this sort is not the privative absence of sound; it involves a self-collection and a listening for some announcement of the encompassing, the mystery that surrounds everyday focal awareness, the mystery of our belonging explicitly to the totality. "Music, in its truth, has always appeared to me as an irresistible call of what, in man, surpasses man, but also founds him" (Life 66).

In this regard, Marcel made a somewhat enigmatic claim that at least points in the direction of the connection he saw between his father's and his own early love of music as a surrogate, though authentic, religion as well as the connection between an appreciation of Bach and his own religious conversion. Prayer he said is "indissolubly wed to silence. It is no doubt for that reason that it is music and also that any music in its profoundest depths is prayer." (Melody 139). *Because it is wed to silence, prayer is music!* The connection is certainly not immediately evident—unless one understands by silence expectant listening for the most basic. And that is precisely what he understands musical listening to be. Great music is an entry into that cohesion and plenitude underlying the scattered and empty that is found on the surface of life.

Marcel's philosophy is founded upon musical reality that suggested to him the categories with which to speak about being as a whole and our relationship to it. In its deepest manifestations it articulates a sense of belonging to the Whole in a feeling of participation that undercuts and grounds the division of faculties. This philosophy speaks out of a sense of universal inter-subjectivity grounded in a relation to the Whole that culminates in the silence of prayer.

There is an additional aspect of the relation between philosophy and music in Marcel. He sees a certain music arising from philosophic success.[67] As in music, there is, at the ground of philosophic thought, a felt sense of attunement, a sense, not a concept, of cohesion and plenitude which answers to our fundamental ontological exigency. Like music, it appeals to a concrete *we*; it involves a sense which carries with it the conviction that it could, in principle, be shared by any other person. Conceptualization is led by that sense. Typically philosophy is focused upon conceptualization, inference and argumentation. Typically also it has failed to ponder its own guiding sensibility. In its speculative form, philosophy has sought a vision of the Whole expressed in a coherent set of concepts. Marcel calls attention to a sense of anticipated cohesion and plenitude which guides that attempt and a sense of fulfillment that attends successful conceptualization.

5.

Marcel's high placement of music has its more proximate historical antecedents in the rise of so-called "absolute music" in the wake of Kant's 1790 *Critique of Judgment*. But it has its more remote antecedents in Plato and Aristotle.

He is close to the notion of the erotic in Plato which draws the lover outside himself and can be sublimated into progressively broader and

higher relationships. Ultimately for Plato, insight into the connected-
ness of the logos depends upon the light generated by erotic ascent
toward the Good which lies beyond the correlation of intellect and
the intelligible.[68] It is this that permits the emergence of the mystical in neo-Platonism and in the Christian tradition stemming from
neo-Platonism.[69] I am not convinced that this is foreign to Plato
where the Good as incomparable Beauty, object of *eros* rather than
of *nous*, generates the light of intelligibility. It is the Phrygian music
of Dionysian eros rather than the Doric music of the soul in the city
that turns us toward the divine.[70]

For Aristotle, music is the most imitative of the art forms. What
is imitative is not the sound but the *ethos*, the feeling produced by
musical sound. *Ethos* itself is the felt proclivity to behave, so that
ethics itself is about feeling aright regarding good and bad.[71] In this
respect Marcel joins the tradition of Aristotle, though Aristotle seems
far removed from the erotic relation to the Whole common to both
Plato and Marcel.

But it is in Kant that the modern tradition Marcel explicitly identifies with had its origin. Kant's notion of form apart from content as
exhibiting the essence of the beautiful[72] and his reference to music as
presenting a whole of feeling of indescribable plenitude[73] was nonetheless linked in his mind to the relegation of music to the lowest level of
the beautiful precisely by reason of its dissociability from non-musical
content expressible in words.[74] As a contemporary of Kant, Sulzer
viewed music as "a civil and entertaining chatter."[75]

However, in the wake of Kant, there occurred a paradigm shift.[76]
German Romantics like Tieck, Wackenroder, Novalis, and Hoffmann
reinterpreted Kant's observations on the dissociation of music from
non-musical content, his focus upon form, and music's presentation
of an indescribable whole of feeling—i.e. music as absolved from the
everyday and rational associations. For them this so-called "absolute
music" expressed the spirit's longing for the infinite, for that which
lay beyond the determinate objects of experience as an encompassing of all finitude. They were guided in this reinterpretation by the
notion of the ineffable that had arisen in connection with poetry. In
Schleiermacher we find the notion of an art religion rooted in the
feelings evoked by music.[77] Poets like Schiller claimed that it is the

musical mood that generates the word, and the full title of Nietzsche's early work was *The Birth of Tragedy Out of the Spirit of Music*.[78] Edgar Allen Poe gives a concrete description of the coming into being of "The Raven" by beginning with a mood of utter despair and searching around for a word that could give expression to that mood. He found it in the word "nevermore"—and so it followed that his lost love came to be named 'Leonore'. All the rest, Poe said, is the creaking of the stage machinery involved in filling out the poem.[79] Walter Pater claimed, as we have previously mentioned, that all art seeks the status of music—only for Pater the sense of participation in the Whole that is articulated in religion is scattered into disconnected fragments of charged aesthetic experiences separated from life.

It was in the atmosphere of a Romantic reappraisal of music that Schopenhauer developed his view of music as the deepest expression of the single underlying Ground of things, the generative desire he called Will which produced the realm of Platonic Ideas that were, in turn, expressed in degenerate form in the world of our ordinary experience.[80] Richard Wagner had first coined the expression 'absolute music' as a derogatory term; but it was Schopenhauer whose thought won him over.[81] After 1870, Wagner, like Schopenhauer, viewed the great sea of harmony as the deeper reality, as the generative source of words and characters in his musical dramas, as the element which joined more familiar shores. It is precisely this metaphor which Marcel invokes. One could also, following Schopenhauer, consider the orthodox Christian notion of the God Father as Origin of the Logos to be pointing to a supra-rational ground.[82] It is also this tradition that Marcel will reinvoke in his notion of music. Just as in the Trinity the Logos lives out of a deeper Ground, so also in human experience the philosophic work of conceptualization lives out of the deeper ground of felt participation in the presence of the encompassing Mystery of Being. It is music which bears witness to that.

Schopenhauer and Hegel were overlapping contemporaries. As he is close to Schopenhauer in several ways, Marcel is also in several ways close to Hegel. Early in his career, Marcel was attracted to Hegel and to the Hegelianism of Bradley.[83] Many of the notions Marcel works with find strong affinities with Hegel's more abstractly and systematically expressed thought. Marcel's notion that the borders of the self extend to all with which one identifies parallels Hegel's notion that personal identity is only achieved through recognition and identification with what is other. The basic notion of identity-in-difference that suffuses the *Science of Logic* provides the categorial structure that underpins Marcel's observations on participation. And Marcel's emphasis upon feeling and "magic" as in some way the soul itself fits with Hegel's notion of the heart as the depth dimension of individual subjectivity linked to the universality of Reason. Raising of the heart to universality and the assimilation of the universal to the heart is the core of human authenticity. Reason without heart and heart without reason are equally inauthentic. It is the arts that effect the mediation of human life, bridging the gap between the abstractness of reason on the one hand and the particularity of the work and the subjectivity of the heart affected by it on the other. Music in that regard stands higher than the plastic arts as expressive of deeper inwardness. However, Hegel argues for the superiority of poetry over music because of its greater proximity to the word which reaches its fullness in explicitly developed Reason. But the dialectical relation with art in general and music in particular calls for a continual reciprocal grounding of art and philosophy.[84]

Of course, for Marcel music transcends what can be attained to conceptually. Reason does not have the last word. It is suspended in and embraced by our relation to the encompassing mystery revealed in the highest forms of music. The mystery of Being is the ground of metaphysics.

* * *

One might think of a philosopher as a person holed up in an room, isolated from other persons and from the natural environment, unconcerned with his embodiment, and surrounded by the books of others long dead. Marcel's philosophy is poles removed from that. A philosophy guided by music is a philosophy guided by a feeling of participation that gives a sense of cohesion and plenitude in principle shareable by any well-disposed human being. It opens out to a recollective mode of reflection that returns the abstractions of philosophy and science to the lifeworld, suggesting categories that point to that return. But music already achieves that in a lived mode. An existential philosophy in the manner of Marcel clarifies such participative feeling to itself and locates it in the Whole. A philosophy rooted in music recalls philosophic reflection itself to lived fullness.

Institute of Philosophic Studies
University of Dallas

Notes

[1] TWB, 231.

[2] TWB, 238-40. See my "The Dialogical Principle and the Mystery of Being: The Enduring Relevance of Martin Buber and Gabriel Marcel," *International Journal for Philosophy of Religion*, vol. 45, no. 2 (April, 1999), 83-97.

[3] *Existential Background of Human Dignity*, Cambridge: Harvard University Press, 1963, p. 21 (henceforth EB). This is Marcel's most accessible and comprehensive treatment of his philosophy.

[4] EB, 50.

[5] On "ontological weight," see EB, pp. 63, 74, and 79; on "participation," EB 18-34 and *The Mystery of Being*, trans. G. Fraser (Chicago: Regnery, 1960) vol. I, 127-153 (henceforth MB I); on "feeling," also MB I, 127-153 ; on "inter-subjectivity," MB I, 210-241; on "hope," *Homo Viator*, trans. E Craufurd (New York: Harper, 1962) (henceforth HV); on "creative fidelity," *Creative Fidelity*, trans. R. Rostal (New York: Noonday, 1964), especially 147-174 (henceforth CF) and EB, 54-74.

[6] On "lived body and body-object," see MB I, 113-126 and EB, p. 46 as well as CF), 24ff; on "problem and mystery," MB I, pp. 251ff and *Being and Having*, New York: Harper and Row, 1965, 100ff; on primary and secondary reflection, MB, I, 95ff.

[7] TWB, 230.

[8] EB, 111.

[9] TWB, p. 231.

[10] EB 18-34. Participation is the first notion treated in this recapitulation of his thought in 1963.

[11] CF 11-37.

[12] MB I, 127-153.

[13] MB I, 123.

[14] MB I, 113.

[15] HV 69.

[16] See "The Mystery of the Family" in HV 68-97; Aristotle, *Politics*, I, 1252a 27; Hegel, *Philosophy of Right*, trans. T. Knox (London: Oxford, 1952), #158-181, 110-122.

[17] See CF 147-174 and EB 54-74.

[18] "On the Ontological Mystery," in PE 13.
[19] MB II, 141. See BH 31 where Marcel claims that "to pray to God is without any question the only way to think of God."
[20] EB, 82-3
[21] PE, 9-46.
[22] Ibid. and MB I, 251.
[23] EB 83.
[24] MB I 22-47; see his play, "The Broken World" (*Le monde cassé*).
[25] EB 86.
[26] A 172. On the "forgottenness of Being," see Martin Heidegger, *Letter on Humanism*, in *Basic Writings*, trans. D. Krell (New York: Harper, 1977), 218; on "the house of Being," Ibid., 193.
[27] PE, 116.
[28] EB 26.
[29] BH, 136.
[30] EB 31.
[31] A 239.
[32] A 57-8.
[33] A 213.
[34] A 229.
[35] A 225.
[36] A 126.
[37] The CD is entitled *Gabriel Marcel: Philosophe et musicien* put out by *Les compagnons d'Orphée*, 8, rue Delambre, 75014 Paris. It contains works by various poets set to music by Debussy, Fauré, and Saroglou as well as by Marcel himself. It is available through tmichaud@wju.edu.
[38] A 175-7.
[39] EB 51.
[40] EB 26.
[41] EB 51.
[42] *The Renaissance* in *Selected Writings of Walter Pater*, ed. Harold Bloom (New York: Columbia University Press, 1974), 55-57.
[43] John Dewey, *Art as Experience*, (New York: Capricorn 1934) 123.
[44] PE 105.
[45] *The World as Will and Representation*, trans. E. Payne (New York: Dover, 1966) I, 4, #28, 153ff; II, 3, #34, 408 (henceforth WWR).
[46] EB 26. Cf. Kant's view of the subjective universality of the feeling of the beautiful in CJ #8, 57-60.
[47] PE, 107.
[48] A 239.
[49] TWB, 222.
[50] Cf. Stephan Strasser, *Phenomenology of Feeling: An Essay on the Phenomena of the Heart*, trans. with an introduction by R. Wood (New York: Humanities Press, 1977).

[51] A 152.

[52] BH 20.

[53] Martin Heidegger, *Introduction to Metaphysics*, trans. G. Fried and R. Polt (New Haven: Yale University Press, 2000), 28.

[54] Roman Ingarden, *The Work of Music and the Problem of Its Identity*, trans. A. Czerniawski, ed. J. Harrell (Berkeley: University of California Press, 1986.

[55] Ibid., 145-149.

[56] Suzanne Langer, *Feeling and Form* (New York: Scribners, 1953), 28.

[57] Jacques Maritain, *Creative Intuition in Art and Poetry* (Princeton: Princeton University Press, 1953), 106-111.

[58] See BH 217.

[59] Martin Heidegger, *Origin of the Work of Art* in *Poetry, Language, and Thought*, trans. A. Hofstadter (New York: Harper, 1968).

[60] *Metaphysical Journal*, trans. B. Wall (Chicago: Regnery, 1952), 276.

[61] Ibid. 277.

[62] EB, 50.

[63] BH 69-74.

[64] On the Open and on Rilke's "inner cosmic space" see Heidegger's "What Are Poets for?" in PLT, 91-142.

[65] EB, 156. See Marcel's treatment of Rilke in *Homo Viator*, 213-270.

[66] *The World of Silence* (Chicago: Regnery, 1956). See my "Silence, Being, and the Between: Picard, Heidegger, Buber" in *Man and World*.

[67] MB I, 95.

[68] *Republic* VI, 508; *Symposium,* 210ff.

[69] Plotinus, *Enneads*, VI, 7, 34.

[70] See my forthcoming "Would Plato Appreciate Abstract Art?" and "Plato's Phrygian Music."

[71] *Politics*, VIII, 4, 1340a 15.

[72] Immanuel Kant, *Critique of Judgment*, ##13-14, trans. W. Pluhar (Indianpolis: Hackett, 1987), 8-72 (henceforth CJ).

[73] CJ, #53, 199.

[74] Ibid.

[75] IAM, 4.

[76] IAM, p. 7.

[77] IAM, 86-7.

[78] Friedrich Nietzsche, *The Birth of Tragedy*, trans. W. Kaufmann (New York: Vintage, 1967), V, 49.

[79] "The Philosophy of Composition," in *Selected Poetry and Prose of Edgar Allen Poe*, ed. T. Mabbott (New York: Modern Library, 1951), 363-374.

[80] WWI, I, 3, #52, 257.

[81] IAM, 19 ff.

[82] On the views of music of Kant and Schopenhauer, see my *Placing Aesthetics*, ch. V and VII.

[83] EB, 9-22.

[84] See my "Hegel and the Heart" in *International Philosophical Quarterly* (June, 2001), and the chapter on Hegel in *Placing Aesthetics* as well as "The Enduring Relevance of Buber and Marcel".

Music in My Life and My Work[1]

...Literature has been the subject of my reveries these past days....
Reverie? It is rather that kind of half-emotional memory that is like a music not yet articulated, an indistinct call towards the other music, the true music...the one that ensured for my thought its most authentic framework. For in the end it is very clear for me today that J.-S. Bach has been in my life what neither Pascal nor Saint Augustine, nor any spiritual writer has been; that I found in the Beethoven or the Mozart of the sonatas and Quartets, or in an infinity of others, from the German Romantics to the Russians and the Spanish, from Rameau to Fauré and Debussy, what no writer has ever given me...[2]

When you so kindly asked me to come give a lecture in the city of Vienna, which, even though it has become familiar, keeps and will always keep its prestige for me, I quite naturally thought that I would speak of what music has been for me in the course of my entire life, not only on the surface but in depth, even if, in order to express myself on such a subject, I had to undertake a veritable interior foraging, by which I mean digging beneath the appearances of everyday life.

Whatever one may say, the fact of growing old constitutes for the human creature a cruel trial, first of all because it means inevitably surviving those who are often for us the dearest, those whose disappearance mutilates us, wounds us to such a degree in our integrity that from that point on we feel forever weakened. But one of the rare compensations for this wound takes place at the level of a certain knowledge—not always, but at least for those who, all their lives, have given much time to reflection.

If I judge from my own experience, I would be inclined to say that the person who grows old, when he turns back towards his past, sees the different levels separate themselves ever more distinctly, like one who, after having walked for a long time in deep valleys, as he gets higher, sees distinctly the different mountain chains between which he has been walking without seeing them. When I try to look at my past life in this way, I note that music has not only played a great role, it has been one of the original components of my very being.

One of my first memories—and at that an indistinct one—is in the apartment of the *Rue du Général-Foy* where I has born, a little way up from the church of St. Augustine, my mother playing piano for my father who was passionately fond of music. No doubt I was playing, but at the same time I was listening. I must have been three at that time. There are even names of musicians, today more or less forgotten—for example, Moschelles and Stephen Heller, whose names I then heard mentioned for the first time, and who take their place in this first stratum of my conscious life. There was also Saint-Saëns. And I mention these names because they were to be eclipsed by the great ones, the major stars of music. Perhaps I heard my father sing as early as this period. He had a fine baritone voice, but it was only several years later that I became aware of this particular gift of his. Later on I even occasionally accompanied him on the piano.

On November 15, 1893—I was nearly four—my mother passed away after only a two-day illness, the result of a chill contracted as she was coming home from the Opéra-Comique. For my father there could be no question of taking care of a little child, so my maternal grandmother and my aunt welcomed me into their apartment on the *Rue Meissonnier*. From this point on my memories become much more distinct. This one, for example: I would sometimes pay a visit to my father in his apartment in the *Rue du Général-Foy* that had been the place of so much happiness. One day I asked to be allowed to take some sheet music just in order to have it with me: it was the *Don Giovanni* of Mozart. I was certainly incapable of reading this sheet music, but it was like a tutelary presence that I needed. At the house on the *Rue Meissonnier* the people there were scarcely music lovers. My aunt was not only remarkably intelligent, but endowed with a real poetic gift. On the other hand, in spite of persistent efforts, she remained forever impermeable to music. Nevertheless, she played piano; and she it was who first had me listen to the sonatas of Mozart and Beethoven.

After she had married my father, three years after the death of her sister, she made persistent efforts to penetrate into this world of music that for her was more or less a closed book. It is thus that she took lessons on the *Ring Cycle* and *Parsifal* from Alfred Bachelet, a musician who was to become famous much later. I would sometimes be present, and I remember the strange trembling this music caused in me, a mere seven year old, a music so different from the kind to which I was otherwise being introduced. Soon a lady friend of my aunt, a cousin of Paul Dukas, was asked to give me piano lessons.

This lady soon realized that my fingering was at best average and that in no case would I ever be able to become a great performer. But she also saw that I was a good reader and that I had an ardent curiosity; and so she tried to get me to decipher the great classical works by playing along with her. I remember quite clearly the stages I went through in succession: Mozart's sonatas, then the simplest of Bach's preludes, which were a revelation for me. Beethoven's sonatas also—not the last ones, of course. I still remember that the adagio of the *Pathetique* as well as that of the *Appassionata* produced for me an ineffaceable memorial of human suffering that will always remain linked to the death of my mother.

At the expense of a kind of division of myself, I am trying to imagine the child that I was then, to make him stand before me, not with any particular self-indulgence. I was an awkward child, timid, overwhelmed by his daily tasks and also by the feeling of a crushing debt towards the one who devoted to him the best of her time and her anxious care, in a large, cheerless apartment that looked out over an impersonal little street of the Plaine Monceau. In a way I was closely tied to the lives of the adults; they spoke freely in my presence and did not neglect any opportunity to instruct me.

But these adults formed a kind of an arch over me. I sadly lacked the brothers and sisters with whom I would have passionately loved to converse or play. A few playmates I was supposed to have fun with in the park of Monceau did not in any way take their place. I think I can say without exaggeration that music was the only escape from this task-filled world.

Of course, there was also the theater. I loved it passionately, but I was taken to it only rarely. The first lyric works that I heard were Gluck's *Iphengenia in Taurus* (in Paris) and *Carmen* (in Stockholm). But what one should perhaps call the life of music in me was developing at another level, the level of intimacy to which my sight-reading, however clumsy, gave access. Until the time when I regularly heard works of chamber music, beginning about 1905 [at age 16], for me concerts played no more than an accessory role compared to this discovery at the piano where the works were revealed to me directly.

Many years later, a graphologist, endowed with an uncommon power of intuition, would say to me, after having studied my writing: "You have in you terrible possibilities of depression; but you get over it very rapidly by two means, nature and music." I was astonished by the precision of his diagnosis, given that he did not know me in the least.

The time spent in Stockholm to which I alluded was very important for the development of my sensibility. In Sweden I felt freed from everything that in Paris was sheer depressing everydayness. I opened myself up to entirely new landscapes, to a northern symphony of water, stone, pines and birches. A certain spontaneous harmony was forming for me between that austere and melancholy natural setting and a certain intimate music to which I was awakening at this time, the music of Grieg, who today seems very secondary to me, but especially the music of Schumann. Musically it was Schumann who was to be the most solid bond between my father and me, perhaps without our having ever said it to each other. He had a passionate tenderness for the Romantic composer. He was even intending to dedicate a book to him in a series with the publisher Laurens for which, if memory serves me, he was to be the general editor. But he was generous enough to give up this position to the critic Camille Mauclair, whom he had helped at the beginning of his career. Much later he expressed the desire that the musical score for Schumann's *Faust* should be placed beside him in his coffin.

I am sorry for the somewhat scattered character of all these recollections. They are various approaches heading towards something that is peculiarly difficult to reach directly. It would perhaps not be completely false to say that from this time on music constituted for me a kind of communion, the value of which was all the more precious, since my relatives had not given me any religious formation. It would be inexact for that matter to claim that I felt then this absence of religious formation as a lack. I am completely sure that, for example, I never envied those around me who were making their first communion.

In view of the agnostic environment in which I lived, it was scarcely possible that catechism or religious ceremonies should appear to me as anything other than strange survivals of a bygone age. It was only much later that I would become acquainted with Nietzsche's "God is dead"; but in a way everything during my childhood, and even at the beginning of my adolescence, happened as though in fact God were dead.

However, this agnosticism certainly did not contain for my family nor for me, I would say even less for me, the kind of strange self-satisfaction that many other free thinkers around the same period seemed to have felt in their negation and their refusal. For my father, the art that he loved passionately constituted at the outside an acceptable substitute for a religion to which he thought an adult mind could not reasonably adhere. Nevertheless, I am certain that the open wound caused by my mother's death must have allowed a secret zone of despair to persist in him. Moreover, an extreme reticence, that I reproached myself for having misunderstood, kept him from letting anyone, save perhaps for my aunt, penetrate into this kind of sanctuary where I am now convinced a vigil lamp remained lit until the end of his life.

With my aunt, profoundly marked by her reading of the French pessimist poets, from Vigny to Jean Lahor and Madame Ackermann, the dissatisfaction was even deeper and more explicit. In her eyes only religion could have made the world tolerable; but, on the other hand, belief seemed impossible for her. This unavoidable contradiction could be resolved only by means of action—action for others, for the most unfortunate, the most dispossessed.

In this desert-like climate it was as though I could scarcely breathe. And, although I cannot say anything with certainty, it seemed to me that in this domain, outside of all possible confirmation, outside of all possible verification, this experience I had of music provided me with a mysterious assurance, as it were, the contents of which, of course, it would have been radically impossible for me to formulate at the time.

A quarter century later, after my conversion to Catholicism [1929], in my book *Être et Avoir,* I spoke of a blind intuition, an intuition, as I have said, that in some way as it were acted upon me and over which I had absolutely no control. It seems to me even that I was gifted with this intuition by music, by what I would like to call musical certitude. I would be strongly tempted to say, without once again being able to affirm anything categorically, that it was with music as a starting point that I was led to reflect on Being or to affirm Being.

This has a negative aspect on which it seems to me very important to focus attention. It was not starting from a visual datum, of whatever nature, that the ontological quest developed in me, but much rather, starting from an experience that it is extremely difficult to translate into a language mostly developed from objects, from things. And may I say in passing, one of the points on which the encounter with Bergson's thought has always been the most fruitful, the most enriching, is precisely this sort of methodical denunciation of the illusions to which language can give rise.

To the preceding can be attached the fact that, at the time of life when ordinarily one awakens to poetry, I turned naturally towards the most musical poetry, the kind closest to music. As it happens, I was quickly disappointed with what French symbolist poetry was able to provide. At the time of which I am speaking, my knowledge of foreign languages was not sufficient to allow me direct access to the highest English or German poetry. A little later on this situation was to change.

You will not be astonished therefore that I was able to consider at one point (I had just turned fourteen or fifteen) the idea of devoting myself entirely to music, to musical composition. My parents would certainly not have been opposed to it. I even learned indirectly a few years ago that my father himself would probably have wished it. So what held me back? The fact that my music teacher, when consulted, was distinctly discouraging. To be sure, I was a musician; but nothing proved that I had in me the makings of a composer. Nevertheless, in the light of what I later experienced just after the Second World War, today I am convinced that I could have followed this path. It is certain, however, that the fugue and counterpoint would have given me a lot of trouble.

In any case, it would be a waste of time to take pleasure in dwelling on these unrealized possibilities. On the other hand, I do not think it useless to attempt to show that my path has in fact been that of a musician transplanted into philosophy and into dramatic art. Of course, I became aware of this only very late, and I add that you will not find this interpretation in any of the studies that have been made of me. This can be explained first of all by the fact that the musical compositions to which I will return and which date from the years 1945 and 1947 are known only to a very few friends. They are neither printed nor recorded. But even if they were more accessible, only a sympathetic understanding would make it possible to see how they provide the key to my work, in so many ways disconcerting and disparate.

The discovery of philosophy in 1905-6 put an end to my hesitations. I was convinced at once that I would be a philosopher and teacher of philosophy. I entered into philosophy somewhat as one enters into religious life: with fervor, with a sacred emotion.

But what is philosophy for me? More or less exactly the opposite of what it may be for a positivist or more generally a mind that comes to it from the direction of the sciences. I will say without hesitation that what I was hoping to get from philosophy was an opening toward what is above.

As I indicated above, those of my classmates and even members of my family who practiced their religion did not seem to me in any way enviable. But I nonetheless aspired with my whole being to raise myself to the heights of speculation, to clear a path for myself that would be my personal path toward the supreme realities: God and immortality.

For that matter, I could not admit that these matters were postulates of practical reason. It seemed to me that I had started off on a path that could only lead far beyond pantheism—like a station through which an express train passes without stopping. The philosophers it was necessary to understand and meditate upon were the great successors to Kant, amongst whom I was little inclined to admit Schopenhauer, whose views on specific matters I admired much more than his general tendency. Curiously, neither Schopenhauer's theory of music nor even Wagner's musical synthesis, considered in its doctrinal aspect, seemed especially to have held my attention at this time. Music was for me essentially a well-spring of thought much more than matter for reflection. I would be inclined to say that it was too active in the very movement of my thought to be able to become its object. But to

express myself thus is to show the almost insurmountable difficulty
of the enterprise I am attempting here.

This difficulty consists in the fact that it is almost impossible to
express in conceptual language this secret activity of music within a
thought passionately engaged in a metaphysical quest, that is to say
thought bearing upon Being. Perhaps I would make myself better
understood if I emphasized the two following points: on the one hand,
music is bearer of truth, on the other hand, much more mysteriously,
it is victory over death.

When I saw that music is truth-bearing, I am aiming above all at
the fact—a negative one—that music, precisely where it frees all the
powers that are in it, does not consist only in affecting us in a certain
way. But neither is it assimilable to a game, to a gratuitous deploy-
ment of forms, although it can quite often be reduced that. On the
other hand, it is very obvious that it cannot be used as a means for
making us conceive certain ideas. As a character in my play *Le Dard*,
the singer Werner Schnee says, "*Music is not an instrument. It has its
value in itself, a value greater than all ideas.*" It is of its essence to be
its own end.

What then does the expression "truth-bearing" mean? Had I been
asked that earlier, I would scarcely have been capable of answering
other than by referring to examples, and I would have borrowed them
principally from the last period of Beethoven's art. Today, however, I
would like to attempt to go beyond examples.

I would like to refer to the distinction that a philosopher such as
Maurice Blondel has established between thinking thought (*pensée pensante*) and thought thought (*pensée pensée*)—incidentally, a distinction
that recalls the one made by Spinoza between naturing nature (*natura
naturans*) and natured nature (*natura naturata*). In an analogous way
I will distinguish between Truth and truths.

The latter, which can be expressed in intelligible terms and also
cannot be separated from the discursive language in which they are
presented, have absolutely nothing to do with music; they belong to
the order of thought that is thought about. The Truth, on the contrary,
can only be subject and this means that it is light, that it is illuminat-

ing, that it is spirit; in fact, it is only to this degree that it can justify all sacrifices, even that of life.

But you will surely ask me what relationship there can be between this Truth which is light, this Truth which is spirit, and a musical expression of any kind. I will answer that one must first pay close attention to ambiguities in the term 'expression' that normally implies a certain distance between the thing expressed and the techniques used to communicate it. It seems to me obvious that in music this distance is absolutely abolished. In addition, it is for this reason that one is justified in questioning whether music can express feelings—which in no way means that it has nothing to do with feeling. On the contrary, music is in a sense feeling itself, but feeling that has managed to free itself so radically from the psycho-somatic matrix in which it is normally trapped that it clarifies itself to the point of becoming structure—structure in time and above time.

I will take as an example the Arietta theme of Beethoven's sonata opus 111. I will not hesitate to say that this theme is mercy itself, beyond all the expression of compassion that could be uttered by the human voice. What one would need to show, beginning with music, is the kind of metamorphosis by which this compassion, reaching its own summit, is transformed into jubilation, a jubilation that nonetheless derives from a persistent suffering that is, as it were, its root in the physical world. Here the *durch Leiden Freude*, as in so many other places in Beethoven, becomes incarnate to the point of visibility.

Let no one object that this is a purely subjective interpretation. What is subjective, what is personal, is the words that each listener tries to use to translate that which transcends all language. In any case, I am not proposing here to give even an outline of a general theory of music. I am trying to bring out how musical experience has irrigated my thought.

To speak of music as a victory over death is in reality to express the same thought. It is not enough to say that music is a means of access to the eternal; that would be misleading. One must say that it is a transmutation by which life simply lived becomes thinking or, more exactly, illuminating in such a way that the other recognizes himself in it beyond all the changes, all the destructions of what we call history.

The connection to the other here is not contingent; on the contrary, it is essential—on condition, of course, that the other himself not be apprehended as object but as Thou. Here we are at the heart of that intersubjectivity toward which, beginning in 1918, my thought has been directed. Furthermore, what is remarkable is that, without my knowing it, others a little before and contemporaneous with me were pursing an investigation that is identical in certain respects: Ferdinand Ebner in Vienna, Martin Buber, and also Max Scheler.

Meanwhile, I was making one musical discovery after another: Wagner, of course, and César Franck, the Russians, and, perhaps even more, contemporary French composers. In the same way that the literary work of the period that was to mark me the most deeply (I mean [Proust's] *la Reserche du temps perdu*), so [Debussy's] *Pelleas* did not reveal itself to me straightaway. I recall very well, after having heard it for the first time, saying that I could not manage to distinguish the exact role of music in a performance that had produced in me a deep but indistinct impression. This was in 1906. A few months later, for something to do during a sea-side vacation imposed on me for health reasons, my father presented me with the sheet music of *Pelleas* and my aunt gave me the music of [Dukas'] *Ariane et Barbe-Bleue*. I was able to rent a piano that was installed in my hotel room; it was an enchanting experience that has never left me. I had no trouble sight-reading the music for *Pelleas*, and I was literally intoxicated by it. It is perhaps the only music that I know by heart, and my admiration for it has never flagged. I also sight-read all the art-songs of Debussy: the poems of Baudelaire, the *Proses lyriques,* the *Fête galantes*. All of that awakened in me an immediate response. I also mention *Ariane et Barbe-Bleue*. I had been present with my father at the dress-rehearsal of this magnificent work that one no longer gets to hear nowadays; this also had a profound influence on me. I am thinking here above all of the final scene in which Ariane, after having freed the captive women, discovers that they are not ready for liberty, and sings to them a fairwell in which disappointment is mingled with an inexpressible melancholy. This music, so different from Debussy's, spoke to what I can call my intellectual sensibility, a sensibility that would be affected more and more deeply by the last works of Beethoven, his quartets, that even today remain for me the summits of musical art.

But how could I not mention as well the indelible impression that Bach's *Passions* and *Cantatas* made on me? I can say without any exaggeration, I think, that they, infinitely more than the *Pensées* of Pascal, started me on the road to conversion.

In this brief attempt to recall my musical journey, there is another name that I want to mention with a fervent gratitude: that of Gabriel Fauré. After the art songs and *Penelope*, which I heard on the eve of the First World War, it is the works of chamber music of the last period, the two quintets, the trio, the two sonatas for piano and cello, and the second sonata for piano and violin that revealed to me the extraordinary genius, still so insufficiently recognized, who managed to incorporate the pure element of eternal Greece into French music.

What a strange eclecticism, you will no doubt say.... I vehemently protest against those who claim that it is not possible to love at the same time the last quartets of Beethoven and the *Missa Solemnis* and *Pelleas* and *la Mer*. My example is there to show that these incompatibilities do not exist. Thank God, I will add, for narrowness and exclusivity have always horrified me. It is a matter of sadness for me to note that the most recent developments in music remain unfortunately foreign to me, like those of painting for that matter. I would we lying if I did not admit it. Nothing would strike me as more dishonest than to feign an admiration or an interest that I did not feel.

I should mention here that, from since I was eighteen or nineteen, I have scarcely ever given up improvising on the piano. It was an uplifting experience, and one that is very difficult to translate into words. Of course, these improvisations were often of a very mediocre quality, being at that time simple, more or less successful pastiches. But it has occasionally happened to me that a barrier was broken through and I then had the feeling of gaining entrance into myself and at the same time of evolving, with an ease that astonished me, inside an unknown world in which the possibilities of discovery were seemingly inexhaustible.

There was yet more. And here I am getting back to what is doubtless the most irreducible element in my dramatic and philosophical work. Truly everything took place as if the frontier between the living and the dead were disappearing, as if I were penetrating into a universe in which this, dare I say, habitual contrast were being radically abolished.

It was, moreover, in those moments that the world 'liberty' took on for me its most authentic meaning. This liberty was creation in its pure state. But strangely at the same time I was experiencing this creation as a grace. There too the traditional frontiers were disappearing.

This extraordinary experience never lasted very long. The barrier re-established itself; I fell back. My wife, my incomparable companion who has known and understood everything about me, was almost the only witness to this ordered delirium. She was almost the only witness—however, not quite the only one. A friend, whom it would be indiscreet to name here, was to hear some of my best improvisations on the piano at her place in the countryside in 1945 and to exhort my wife to get them down on paper. My wife possessed in fact the technical abilities that I was lacking, and it is thanks to her alone that the very numerous art songs I composed were able to take shape. I do not at all mean that she harmonized them, for the musical phrases have always been given to me together with their harmony. I refer here only to the problem of transcription, which could not have been solved without her. It was an astonishing blaze of inspiration that came to an end, alas, in 1947, with her death.

The poems for which I wrote music are quite diverse. I will mention here only the main ones: Du Bellay's *Complainte du désespéré*, André Chénier's *Mes mânes à Clytie*, Lamartine's *le Lac,* three pieces by Baudelaire, including *Mosta et errabunda*, the *Cimetièrre marin* and several short pieces by Paul Valéry, nine poems by Supervielle, three pieces by Patrice de La Tour du Pin, etc. I also set to music, in the original German, of course, a few poems by Rilke, Hölderlin's *Song of Hyperion*, the *Die Ballade des aüßeren Lebens* by Hoffmannsthal.

A certain number of these art songs have been sung on the radio or elsewhere, sometimes by such fine performers as Jean Giraudeau and Paul Derenne. Nevertheless, all that remains practically unknown. However, I will say without the least hesitation that these art songs must appear someday in an edition of my complete works. I am convinced that those capable of understanding them will find in them, as it were, a light that enlightens the most personal and most secret aspects of my work. I am thinking here both of my essential philosophical writings and my plays.

The philosophical writings: Has my endeavor not consisted to a large degree in freeing myself as much as possible from the categories of the observed world to guarantee for myself presences that never free themselves more perfectly than in song? On this level my thought continues in the tradition of Schopenhauer of whom I was speaking above. Of course, I admit his pessimism, against which I have always protested, without ever forgetting that the world does seem, on all sides, to invite us to despair. But as I have already said, it seems to me that it is music and music alone that has caused me to discover the saving light. It is music that has opened the road to Truth for me, towards which I have not ceased striving, this Truth beyond all the partial truths that science demonstrates and expounds, the Truth that illumines the work of the greatest composers like Bach or Mozart.

But my theater itself is musical in its very essence, no doubt about it. Ramon Fernandez, reviewing "A Man of God" *(Un homme de Dieu)* around 1925, noted with a rare penetration, that this play seemed to him musically conceived. It is not by chance that in one of my first plays, the *Quartet in F Sharp*, published immediately after the First World War, music is the protagonist.

In this play, when the curtain rises, one hears the last lingering chords that end the quartet. It is a piano quartet, of which the string parts are held by Stéphane Mazères, the composer, his brother Roger, and violist Vermandé, while at the piano is a Dutch artist, Doris van Cleef. The performance was held for the old musician Neyrel, Stéphane's teacher. Everyone is anxiously wondering what the the old man's verdict will be. Neyrel, while he expresses some reservations about the first three parts which he does not find very personal, on the other hand recognizes a completely new spirit in the finale.

Neyrel. "Look now, the other parts are good music; the finale is music, period. (At this moment Stéphane cannot help looking at Claire who is frowning.) In all honesty, I would not have thought you capable of doing that. It is not at all the dolorous and rather hackneyed César Franckism of your sonata. And you have to admit it is very far from the rather conventional elegance of your art-songs. Here there is a completely new spirit. I cannot express it any other way. You know this idea that emerges suddenly on the piano after the great arpeggios of the beginning: the cello at once takes hold of it; this idea is a living being. (Gesturing toward Roger.) By the way, your brother played it marvelously. It imposes itself on all these too familiar, too facilely developed themes. It dominates them; it carries them off; it does with them what it pleases; and then it disappears. A kind of mist covers it. In vain everything calls out for it. It refuses the appeals of the strings. And the piano wanders about vainly only to grow quiet in the end, discouraged. And then.... This now is what I think is the most beautiful. This silence, this sudden peace, this resignation in the face of the idea that has disappeared and all the same is still there; for it *is* there; it subsists still in the heart of the regret that it has left behind. (He turns towards Stéphane.) That's more or less it, isn't it?"

But one person seems to be excluded from the harmony which has taken form in this quartet: it is Claire, the composer Stéphane Mazères' own wife. In fact, she does not forgive her husband for the infidelities that he declares to be without importance and that he seems to want to justify by the fact that an artist is not a man like others. Claire has decided to get a divorce and will not let herself be stopped by the exhortations of her mother-in-law who is sorry to see a union come to an end from which she had hoped so much. Stéphane and Claire had a child, but it died. Roger, Stéphane's brother, finds himself torn between his affection for his brother and the tender compassion Claire's bitter grief inspires in him. Even after the divorce has been finalized he continues to see her, without himself knowing exactly what to call what he is feeling: compassion, friendship, love? Claire in any case believes she is in love with him, and, perhaps unduly taking advantage of the fact that Roger is a rather indecisive but profoundly generous person, brings him gradually to the point of proposing marriage. Claire accepts and we can only wonder if error and abuse has not entered into all this.

Roger, having become Claire's second husband, continues to see his brother, to participate in his musical life. Sometimes they even play together and the intransigent Claire grows indignant at Roger's being able to remain thus closely linked to the man who has made her so miserable. Thereby an element of tension is introduced between the spouses—not right away however. Before discovering how close the intimacy between the two men has remained, Claire has experienced moments of happiness and she happens to confide in Doris van Cleef, the Dutch pianist. Claire asks her why so few composers have been able to express happiness, why happiness, in order to be sung, has to sound sorrowful.

Doris: "I don't know... I gave up thinking about music a long time ago."

Claire: "Really?"

Doris: "Maybe because music in my view has nothing to say that has anything to do with life. If you translate it into words...nobody would understand it."

Claire: "You really think so?"

Doris: (growing animated): "I've often thought that everything people have gotten out of the habit of believing, what they no longer have words or respect for—Well! You see, all of that stuff has, so to speak, taken its revenge, in music. Isn't music like the immortality of everything we think is dead but in fact lives on?"

Claire has some difficulty following Doris on this path, but she is fairly itching to speak with her about her first husband, for the young pianist sees the composer on a regular basis. He has just finished a sonata for piano and violin and has chosen her to play it. Still on the subject of happiness, *Claire* states, "There is a happiness that he will never know, I guarantee you. It wouldn't seem fair to me if he did."

"So," *Doris* answers, "You think that people only have the happiness to which they have a right. It's strange... I don't think that at all... 'Deserve' is a school-teacher's word... If deserving were that important, I'm not sure life would be worth living. I remember that when I was little nothing made me sadder than the stories in which the good people were always rewarded and the villains were always punished. I found that so unfair, because, don't you see, either the villains know that they will be punished—and in that case I thought they were really brave to do evil even so, or else they didn't know it—and in that case it was really unfair to trick them like that."

Is all this pure arrogance? Not at all, on the contrary. I will in no way say that Doris is my spokesperson here, but I think she does have a point in bringing out the narrowness of a certain attitude of moral intransigence. It is as though the powerful inspiration of music came and swept away rules that were too rigid and especially a moral Pharisaism that is too quickly satisfied with them.

And yet the play is not a defense of art for art's sake either or anything like that. The point here is not, any more than in my other plays, to demonstrate or to refute but only to show.

Claire is devastated when she notes not only that the two brothers are continuing to see each other, but that Roger claims the full right to remain as close to Stéphane as ever. Claire, on the basis of an abstract logic, claims that this is incompatible with the feeling that Roger claims he has for her. But in reality what kind of feelings exclude each other? All are "compossible"? And one can wonder if the second marriage is not going to collapse like the first. But Claire, giving way to an irresistible impulse, goes and hides at the end of the room in which the *Quartet in F Sharp* is being performed. (The composer has finally given it its definitive form.) Hearing this performance overwhelms her; it brings about in her a kind of conversion, and it is a changed woman who then seeks out Roger and tries to explain to him what has happened in her.

In fact, everything has taken place as if this music allowed her to see herself, to judge and condemn herself. For this music contains not only her own suffering but also something quite different, including Stéphane's impure but at the same time real love for her. Essentially she does not even know any more if she has loved Roger for himself or if he has not been for her simply a reflection of his brother. Moved by an irresistible impulse of sincerity, she reveals all this to Roger; and what is unusual is that this confession brings them together. To be sure, he is sad at the thought that he has perhaps not been loved for himself. But does this expression mean anything?

"Yourself? Himself?" *Claire* asks. "Where does a person begin? It was you all the same. Don't you think that each of us is continued in everything he awakens?"

And *Roger* thinks there is comfort in this thought. "Yes," he says. "Music tells the truth, music alone.... Perhaps deep inside I couldn't forgive you for not having loved him more."

And so a sort of rich and mysterious harmony is created among them because a truth has illuminated them, a truth that music alone is able to provide. As soon as one attempts to translate it into words it withers. And the unusual idea arises in Roger that their union, made fecund by this truth that music bears in itself, will not remain sterile. A light has arisen: why should it not pass some day into a gaze? It's the last line of the play.

Today, thinking critically about this whole play, I will say that in my opinion it contains a serious dramaturgical error. It is asking too much of the spectator that he should imagine on his own what the quartet may mean for Claire, this quartet of which he, the spectator, has heard only a few measures. I do not think that it is legitimate to introduce as a determining factor in a dramatic action a process in which the spectator cannot really participate.

This error can be explained, I think, if not justified. Everything takes place rather as if I, a secret musician as it were, a closet musician, have really composed this quartet, as if it were present in me. But in addition to the fact that this presence was obviously incommunicable, even if I had really written the quartet, it would have been very risky to have it performed on the stage. The author has the right to count only on his own means and should not depend on a hypothetical composer, unless, of course, we are talking about a lyric work as such, which poses quite different problems.

Apart from this reservation (in my opinion a serious one), the play nevertheless remains important within the context of my work considered as a whole. The experience of music as a transforming power—let us say more exactly, as a depository of truth, is without any doubt the kind that can elucidate my philosophical thought, and in particular the fact that my thought is opposed to any attempt to present a visual conception of the real, if I may say so, and rejects any *Weltanschauung* and any *esprit de système*.

But I think especially that it would be appropriate to inquire into the essence of this truth of which music is supposedly the depository. And here above all I no doubt have in mind the great musicians who have lived in this city of Vienna for all or part of their lives. I am thinking of the last quartets of Beethoven, of the final works of Schubert, and especially of the quintet for two cellos. I am also thinking of Brahms, whose work, after a long period of incomprehension, is at last valued in France as it deserves. I can say that, for half a century this idea of a musical truth, of a truth that is revealed in music, has continued to impose itself on me, but I must also confess that I have never managed to elucidate it through a direct approach. On the other hand, I think that the progress of my reflection in the realm of pure philosophy has been entirely governed by this idea. Furthermore, it is certain that the word 'idea' is somewhat misleading here, especially if by this word one means a kind of intellectual object. It could not possibly be a question of anything like that. As is so often the case, here it is necessary to call on the idea of light in contrast to what can be illuminated by this light. For years I have very frequently emphasized the need to distinguish between Truth and truths. Truths, and in particular truths of a scientific order, can be treated as objects if one insists, but only to the degree that we identify them with the propositions in which they are formulated, something, however, that is not perfectly licit. Things are quite different with Truth which, in contrast, is a spirit and which consequently cannot be possessed but can be affirmed only in and by witnesses. It is this spirit that can become incarnate in music. This amounts to saying that I was not expressing myself very precisely when I said a moment ago that music is a depository of truth. What I meant was that it is given to music to communicate to us a Truth that is beyond all abstract formulations, and that is what I tried to show at the end of *Quartet in F Sharp*.

I will mention in passing that this play attracted the attention of Rilke. After his death they found a copy of the play annotated by him, but I attempted in vain to get my hands on it when I visited his house a few years ago. The volume had been misplaced.

I would like to spend a bit of time talking about two other plays in which music plays an important role. First of all *The Dart* (*le Dard*) to which I alluded in passing and which I consider today one of my most significant works. The story takes place at the same time as when the play was written, that is in 1936. Racial persecution has begun in Germany; the German tenor Werner Schnee has maintained his association with his accompanist Rudolf Schönthal. The latter, a Jew, has been beaten, has had to leave Germany, and will soon die in a sanitorium as a result of injuries cased by the Nazis. Werner Schnee, although he is not an Jew, and his wife Gisela have thus also had to leave Germany and quite naturally they have sought a temporary asylum in the environs of Paris at the home of Eustache Soreau, a young professor of German with whom Werner once was associated in Marburg. Though Eustache is a characteristic representative of the leftist intellectuals of that time suffering under a certain generalized resentment, his case is unusual. He comes from a very modest social milieu. A scholarship holder, he did brilliantly on his examinations and subsequently became the son-in-law of a rich and influential politician who has aided his advancement. Everything seems to have turned out well for him. His wife Beatrice, a charming woman, loves him. He is going to be appointed professor in one of the great *lycées* of Paris. But it is precisely his success that he cannot manage to digest because he does not cease to see himself through the eyes of his bitter comrades who accuse him of having become bourgeois, in particular, a certain Gertrude Heuzart, a communist grade school teacher, a previous political comrade-in-arms. Beatrice, who is refined and sensitive, suffers a great deal from realizing that her husband is prey to a guilty conscience that is poisoning him. She confides in Werner Schnee who, because he is a pure artist, knows nothing of such complexes. Gradually the situation between Eustache and Werner grows tense. In the scene I am going to quote, the question is about music. Werner has just sung a brief *Lied* by Hugo Wolf, based on a poem by Goethe, for Eustache and Beatrice and in the presence of his wife Gisela,

Beatrice to Eustache: "What do you think of it, Eustache?"
Eustache (dryly): "I think it's pleasant."
Werner: "What do you mean 'pleasant'? It's got a form, a style. That's the essential, isn't it?"
Eustache: "If you want my opinion, I find it morbid. "
Werner: "What do you mean 'morbid'? How is it morbid?"
Eustache (getting heated): "In this day and age we can no longer get excited about these little refinements."
Werner (simply): "I don't understand."
Eustache: "We need a music that speaks to the masses."
Werner: "You'll need trombones and tubas...."
Eustache: "That kind of music speaks to the idle; it's superfluous. The kind of art I am thinking of must be necessary."
Werner (to Beatrice laughing): "It's funny what he's saying."

Eustache (irritated): "I don't see why."

Werner: "Mozart, for example. What do you think of Mozart?"

Eustache: "Let's not go back to that old subject of discussion. I admit that there is probably something there I am missing."

Werner: "You are actually proud of it." (He bursts out laughing.)

Eustache: "I prefer to speak of what I love and I am sure of appreciating."

Werner: "Maybe you're mistaken there too."

Gisela: "Werner!...."

Eustache: "Beethoven...."

Werner: "I was expecting this. But I'm afraid that there is a mix-up here. You forgive Beethoven...."

Eustache (irritated): "I admire him."

Werner: "On account of his ideology (he pronounces it with a hard 'g'). That has nothing to do with music. Absolutely nothing. You think that music must produce beautiful thoughts. But that isn't true. You also think that it is an instrument for—how do you say it? *Zur Befreiung.*"

Beatrice: "For emancipation."

Werner: "Music is not an instrument. It has a value in itself, a value greater than all ideas. I can't explain it, but I am sure I'm right."

Eustache: "Essentially you are a disciple of art for art's sake. But that's old hat. If art is not integrated into the collective life...."

Werner: "What does that mean? You want to enslave art, put it in the service of the state. You speak like a Nazi, not otherwise." And attacking the deplorable lack of distinction that he finds in Eustache's mind between art and ideology, he cries: "Mozart and Schubert were poor wretches. Sometime they didn't know if they would have anything to eat. Even so, they didn't say 'I must make revolutionary music.'."

"But," replies *Eustache*, "since their day our consciousness has developed."

"What consciousnesss?" *Werner* asks.

Eustache rejects individual charity. "Yes, I am well aware."

Werner cries: "You believe in public welfare. I simply think that it is an office for generalizing a bad disposition. There are people who say: 'If nobody is satisfied everybody will be a little happy' because they will say, 'I'm not very well off, but my neighbor is not very well off either.' I say there will perhaps no longer be any unhappiness, but there will not be any joy either. Everybody will be in a bad mood, and that's the worst thing that can happen! With suffering one can still make music, but not with a bad mood."

And *Eustache* murmurs, "Music! It's very secondary after all."

"No, Eustache," answers *Werner*, "it isn't secondary. If music diminishes, if music becomes poorer, then life itself diminishes; it become stingy. Without music one doesn't live anymore; one is just getting along."

When I re-read this scene a quarter of a century later, I think I have written nothing more significant and with which I agree even more completely today. For if one conviction has grown stronger in my mind in the course these last twenty years, it is that the essential thing in every human being is the role of creation in him, however reduced it may be. And I will add today that the contentment through which it is manifest is expressed or at least previously expressed itself so often in singing. A world in which men no longer sing is a degenerate world. The real problem which is so rarely posed and which is moreover so difficult to resolve is to know if in a given group of human beings contentment remains or on the contrary is being abolished. And it is absolutely not true, as people would have us believe, that the standard of living insofar as it is measurable corresponds to contentment. When I see with consternation the enormous structures people are in the process of building, for example all around Paris, and in which humans will no longer be lodged but simply stuffed, I ask myself fearfully what contentment could persist in such termite colonies. In reality such structures are the terrifying expression of a technocratic thought that no longer considers human beings as individualities, but only as units of profit.

It is against this world that Werner protests. But in Eustache he comes up against a total incomprehension because this unhappy man is incapable of realizing that this world of technocratic socialism may, at the limit, have a strange resemblance to the Nazi totalitarianism that it execrates. Eustache reproaches his friend for not having the attitude that his situation as a refugee requires, for not saying the words appropriate to a refugee—that is to say, as

Werner observes ironically, that one would have to pronounce certain ritualistic words, "my thoughts should put on a uniform, the uniform of the exile. But I hate uniforms, even that one. One must above all remain a human being."

Eustache: "A human being! A human being! A word you seem to relish.... About Rudolf...."

Werner: "I prefer not to speak about Rudolf right now."

Eustache: "Why?" (Werner makes an evasive gesture.) "He had a doctrine; he served a cause; he had been a party member [*il avait adhéré*]...."

Werner: "That's a word that frightens me."

Eustache: "They claim that Frenchmen are individualists."

Werner: "I don't know if it's still true."

Eustache: "I have never seen a Frenchman who was as individualist as you."

Werner: "It's always easy to slap on a label."

Eustache: "Whether you realize it or not, the fact of leaving Germany has categorized you. You have made a choice. You ought all the same to conform to the logic of your acts."

Werner: "What logic?"

Eustache: "You seem to refuse to have any contact with the refugees in Paris. It is as though they didn't inspire any confidence in you."

Werner: "It's a question of personality. Anyway, in general, I don't know them."

Eustache: "It's as though you wanted to maintain your distance. What the devil! Solidarity exists after all."

Werner: "You're right. I am mistrustful."

Of precisely what is he mistrustful? Of all these human groupings who have in common only demand and resentment, or at least in whom demands and resentments end up always concealing what, to begin with, might have been a real human bond, a friendship. What difference is there between this and the communion that is established either among believers or among those who listen together to a beautiful work in which they feel their prayers are mysteriously answered? Nothing suggests that Werner is a believer. But there is in him the idea of the human being that acts as the moving force behind his life, an idea of the human beyond all the differences of class and party. Rudolf Schönthal, his friend, this pianist for whom he left Germany, was a Jew and a communist; but he was first of all a human being, a generous and radiant being. And beyond death he remains a stimulating example for Werner.

But the relationship between Werner and Eustache will continue to grow more tense in as much as Eustache is obscurely jealous of Beatrice's admiration for Werner. In response to Eustache who accuses him of not really having burnt his bridges with the people there, that is to say in Nazi Germany, Werner reveals to him that he has been visited by a kind of impresario, an emissary of the Nazis who told him that if he made certain written promises he could return to Germany and even get work in a theater, perhaps at Magdeburg or at Dessau. Werner sent him on his way. But in no case does he want his wife Gisela to be informed about this visit, for she would be incapable of understanding Werner's refusal, since she maintains that she is not interested in politics and has only one idea, to return to Germany at whatever price. However, Eustache eventually reveals to the young woman what has happened. Werner, indignant at this betrayal, has seated himself at the piano and, with his head lowered, plays a few chords.

Gisela: "Werner, stop tinkering on the piano, it's annoying." (Werner plays a few chords softly.) "Have you seen that fellow Wetzinger? You won't answer me? Well, that's fine. I know now. (To Eustache) Has he told you? (To Werner) Did he propose your returning to Germany? We could have returned to Germany? But maybe it's still not too late."

Werner: "Wetzinger has left."

Gisela: "You admit that he offered you...."

Werner: "I told him no...irrevocably no."

Gisela (in a voice increasingly choked with sobs): "You didn't have the right. You are not alone. I'm here too. I don't want to live like a beggar. I have my family, my house, my own life.... What do I care about politics?"

Beatrice (going up to her): "Gisela, listen to me...."

Gisela: "I'm not an idiot. I won't let myself be sacrificed... Werner! (He doesn't answer but continues playing chords, gazing off into the distance.) Ah! Rudolf has something to do with this... I warn you. I will not spend my life fighting with a dead man. I did not realize that I was the wife of a madman. I will leave, you understand...but not alone. There will be someone else.... *Ein Wahnsinniger....*" (She goes out sobbing.)

(A long silence.)

(Eustache has seated himself at the back of the stage and seems to be deeply absorbed in a book that he took from the table; the two others completely ignore his presence.)

Werner (without turning around): "If there were only the living, Gisela, I think that the earth would be completely uninhabitable."

This last sentence, to which I will return, is without doubt one of the most significant in all my plays. I will limit myself to summarizing in a few words the end of the play.

The rupture is complete. But after some time Werner comes back to say goodbye, not to Eustache but to Beatrice. As he foresaw, Gisela has left with an "admirer". He himself has almost no more money. To be sure, he doesn't lack for kindly people who would be only too happy to take him in. He could thus lead the life of a parasite—not such a bad prospect after all. But it displeases him to "get by on friend-ship"—that is to say, to use for his advantage the fact that people like him. An unusual change has taken place within him. If there is in him something that wins hearts, this strange power must be placed in the service of the unhappy, of the disinherited. He has decided to return to Germany, but not as the impresario would have wished. "I will be arrested. I am counting on being arrested. I have done what is necessary for that. I have spent the last evenings with German com-munists in the cafes. The Nazis are very well informed about it. I am sufficiently compromised." He will thus be sent to a concentration camp and there perhaps he will have the opportunity of bringing some comfort to his unhappy comrades.

The very meaning of this decision he has made is not absolutely clear to him. He is not sure that he is not being contaminated, as it were, by Eustache's guilty conscience. But he now judges Eustache lucidly without animosity. He even feels a sort of compassion for him. To be sure, Eustache has behaved very badly, even with regard to Beatrice.

He has cheated on her with the communist elementary school teacher
and Beatrice seems ready to leave him.

"No, Beatrice," *Werner* declared to her forcefully. "You must not
abandon him. You must always remember that you are the wife of
a poor man. Poverty is not the lack of money or the lack of success.
Eustache has had money; he has had success; he has remained poor,
ever poorer. He will doubtless never be healed of his poverty. It is the
greatest sickness of our time; it spreads like a plague. We have not yet
found a doctor to treat it. We don't even know how to recognize it.
The artist will escape it, no doubt, even if he doesn't eat his fill. And
also the believer, who can pray... All the others are threatened."
   Beatrice: "You're asking me to live with a leper...."
   Werner: "Cases of leprosy are going to multiply on the earth, I fear.
It will be a grace reserved for a very few to live there knowing that
they live among lepers and without being horrified by them. Even
more than a grace. How do you say? 'viaticum'...."
   Beatrice: "I'm not brave enough, Werner, I assure you."
   Werner: "You will think of me as I think of Rudolf. Later I will haunt
you the way Rudolf haunts me. And you will remember then what I
told you a few weeks ago. If there were only the living, Beatrice.... "
   (Curtain)

At the end of the play, then, we find once again the sentence that
I was underscoring just now. It is certain, difficult as it probably is,
to find a fully intelligible justification for this fact that for me, in the
region in which the mind and heart communicate, there has always
existed a close relationship between music and the concrete presence
of those who are called the dead. As I have said elsewhere, as a result
of strictly personal circumstances, it appeared to me from the very
beginning of my philosophical vocation, that I would have to affirm
this presence and, insofar as I was able, to elucidate its nature. But it is
completely certain that, in conditions that can only remain mysterious,
music has always been for me, in the course of this hectic philosophical
quest I have pursued, a permanent guarantee of that reality that I was
attempting to reach by the arid paths of pure reflection.

My original intention when I began to prepare this text was not to dwell as long as I have on *Le Dard*. But upon reflection, this play appeared to me as one of the most significant I have written, if only because of its prophetic character. It is easy to understand, in fact, that this leprosy, this poverty that Werner Schnee speaks about, is the spiritual degradation of those who dehumanize themselves and are no longer anything but cogs in the enormous machine to which technocrats, communists or not, tend to reduce the society of men. Music is the very incarnation of that which, in each one of us, protests against this frightful mutilation.

I may say that my entire work, for the past quarter of a century, has been nothing but the expression of this protest, or, from another point of view, one must see in it the elucidation of the concrete conditions outside of which the human is denatured, is perverted. Music, in its truth, has always appeared to me as an irresistible call of what, in man, surpasses man, but also founds him.

And I will now say, at the risk of scandalizing some people, that, perhaps wrongly, I am afraid of finding in a certain completely contemporary music, the kind that has broken with tonality and that tends to be reduced to an abstract aural experimentation, the same process of dehumanization which manifests itself at the same time in the other arts and in behavior. This fear, or at least this anxious questioning, comes to light in the last play I have written, *My Time Is Not Yours* (*Mon temps n'est pas le vôtre*). It is a complex play that presents itself first under the appearance of a satirical comedy but ends as a tragedy. Here I will consider only one character, the Italian pianist Flavio Romanelli.

Nothing, to be sure, would be more false than to see in him my spokesman. He has some almost ridiculous aspect that must be felt as such; some people have even found him not a little irritating. But some of the words I have placed in his mouth are for me of great significance. This young pianist has composed a concerto for piano and orchestra into which he has put all his heart; but he is perfectly aware that, apart from exceptions of genius, works composed by beginners are not worth much. He anxiously awaits the verdict of a conductor to whom he has submitted his work. In circumstances that I won't elaborate on, he makes contact with a French family in which the two daughters swear only by avant-garde music and are interested only in what doesn't resemble anything. The father of these girls, for that matter, finds them exasperating and feels a deep appreciation for Flavio, who does not hide his reactionary tastes. Here is the end of a scene which puts the pianist in conflict with one of the daughters, the less aggressive of the two, Marie-Henriette. He has just started playing a few measures of the andante of his concerto on the piano for the father. Marie-Henriette enters at this moment.

Marie-Henriette (after having listened for a moment): "What's that? It's wonderful but not very modern."

Flavio (stops, very irritated): "Well, we really like interrupting here, don't we! What's that supposed to mean, 'modern'?"

Marie-Henriette: "O well, I don't know: polytonal, atonal.... What do you think about twelve-tone music?"

Flavio: "I hate it."

Marie-Henriette: "Perhaps you haven't been properly instructed in it."

Flavio: "I am not corrupted."

Marie-Henriette: "You're very sure of yourself."

Flavio: "I'm not sure of myself. I'm sure of Bach. I'm sure of Mozart. I'm sure of God."

Marie-Henriette: "O, God.... He has nothing to do with this."

Flavio: "He certainly does, much more than you think."

Marie-Henriette: "And if it should proved to be the music of the future?"

Flavio (vehemently): "The future! Do you breathe in the future! Do you eat in the future? Just what is the future?"

Marie-Henriette: "Here, you see, we have advanced ideas. I am not speaking about papa, of course."

(Champel has gone out.)

Flavio: "Advanced! [*avancé*] That's what we say in French about game that's beginning to smell bad; that's no reason for pride. Your father has left. I can well believe that he does not take much pleasure in hearing such nonsense."

Marie-Henriette: "*Mine*?"

Flavio: "*I* didn't say anything nonsensical."

Marie-Henriette: "I wonder if you speak this way to your mother or your fiancée."
Flavio: "Fortunately, they don't talk like you."

And a little later, as Marie-Henriette observes that the conductor to whom *Flavio* has sent his concerto is not open to the new music, he cries: "But I congratulate him for that. That's the reason why I sent him my concerto. It's really incredible, this pretension, this vanity of people who know nothing, who feel nothing! When you go to a concert, what are you looking for? One or two idiotic little remarks that you will repeat the next day to your friends in order to impress them. 'Heifetz wasn't in form: he disappointed me the other evening. I find that Horowitz has declined. The *Symphony in B Minor* bores me to death. But *Goat Droppings* by... O, you know... that Ruthenian composer whose name nobody can pronounce. Now that's interesting! *Goat Droppings*, that is extraordinary. Beethoven's *Pathetique* can't even compare to *Goat Droppings*.'"
Marie-Henriette: "You are really outrageous!"
Flavio: "I'm not outrageous, but I can become outrageous, senorina. When people talk to me in a certain way about the most sacred things in the world: art, religion."
And when *Marie-Henriette* observed timidly that "You can't still say in 1955...," *Flavio* exclaims: "The truth is the truth. 1955 is just a number. It doesn't mean anything, any more than the number on a train's meal ticket. 1955! You say that as if it were some height, as if you were on Mt. Everest and were looking down at the bottom of the valley on the poor people who have existed there for centuries. But it isn't true. You are not on Mr. Everest. 1955 is not a height. The men and women of 1955 are on a little insignificant mound—and San Francesco, San Bonaventura and all the others, they are in the stratosphere, in spite of the number."
Thus, what is denounced here with a kind of fury is this rage for novelty at any price, this prejudice in favor of the unusual which, in our days, is allied in such an alarming way with advertising frenzy. Nobody can deny that in the great periods in the history of music the concern for innovation at any price was entirely foreign to the

great creators. This is what *Flavio* says much later in a particularly tragic moment.

"'Novelty' is an advertising word, a merchant's word; but in this interior country, which is my country, nothing is sold anymore, nothing is bought any more; it's the country of contemplation, of grace." And when his fiancée, who has a practical turn of mind, asks him how one lives in this country, since in order to live one must buy bread and a few other indispensable things, he tells her:

"No doubt we must pay tribute to this world, a tribute of money and sin. But to pay a tribute is not the same thing as to sell one's soul. It's just to do an unpleasant and honorable work in order to have the right to contemplate and to create, as the monks understood."

Marie-Henriette then observes that all the great artists have brought something new: "In spite of themselves!" cries *Flavio*, "without ever wanting it, without ever having said to themselves: now what could I invent that would be new and interesting...? Often with anguish, with remorse, and only because they didn't have any other way of expressing the eternal essence that was the goal of their inward fervor. But today it's because this goal has disappeared, because the eternal essence is no longer perceived by anybody—that crazy people invent anything whatever to replace it or to help forget it, as though the eternal were replaceable, as if the eternal were forgettable!"

To these quotations which in fact do not give a precise idea of the play, I would like to add two remarks.

In the first place, neither I nor anybody else knows that value of Flavio's concerto which, in the end, does not get performed. It may very well be that my young pianist is only a sort of lesser Rachmaninoff. The question remains the same. One can write, in all sincerity, with all fervor, music that the experts and up to date people declare out of date: is this music contemptible because of it?

The second remark has to do with contemporary music. I certainly don't have the right simply to condemn it because composers like Boulez or others of his generation bore or irritate me. But what appears to me absolutely certain is at the very least that music has gotten on a slippery slope, that of the worst kind of experimentation; and for that reason it ceases to be addressed to everybody. I will recall here what a character said in my play "The Broken World" ("*Le monde cassé*"), written almost thirty years ago:

"Don't you sometimes have the impression of living—if you can call it living—in a broken world—you know, the world, the world of men? Formerly it must have had a heart. But it seems like that heart has stopped beating."

Trying to define for myself what seems to me to have been my task for many years and to uncover the meaning of the innumerable encounters it has been given me to have day after day with people from all the continents, it is the expression of '*auscultation*' or '*stethoscoping*' that presents itself naturally to my mind. If one wished to define me, it seems to me that instead of speaking of me as an existentialist philosopher (a pretentious expression and one that, in the last analysis, is almost empty of meaning), you would have to say quite simply that I am, above all, a listener.

Notes

[1] This piece was originally the text of a lecture given in Vienna on September 25, 1959, and in Brussels on October 15, 1959. Subsequently Gabriel Marcel took certain passages from it and with additions developed an article entitled "Aperçus sur la musique dans ma vie et mon ouervre" that appeared in *Livre de France* in August/September 1965.

[2] Extract from an article by Gabriel Marcel that appeared June 17, 1948 in *Nouvelles Litérraires* after he had won the Grand Prix de Littérature.

Reflections on the Nature of Musical Ideas: The Musical Idea in César Franck

In the following few pages we would like to attempt to determine the characteristics of a living musical idea, to show how general reflections of this order can be made precise by the study of Franck's "musical phrase".

Nothing in music can, I believe, give a more complete aesthetic certitude than the first measures of the *Quartet in D* or the sublime descending phrase in the second part of the *Chorale in A*. Aesthetic certitude, I have said: the coupling of these two words may be surprising, I admit. It corresponds, however, to an inner experience of which there could be no question of purely and simply rejecting. In spite of the claims of an indolent subjectivism whose principle concern is to avoid all controversy, there is certainly no verb that expresses the pure aesthetic emotion less well than the word "to please" (*plaire*). The beautiful is what, in a certain way, has authority over us. Authority is the distinguishing mark of a work of art, whether it is exercised immediately or not, whether it must struggle or not with a rebellious sensibility. And this helps us to understand what is, without doubt, the most important distinction that can be made in the aesthetic order: the distinction between what *exists* and what doesn't exist. The non-existent is what does not possess in itself any power of affirmation and consequently has no authority over us. Hence one sees that the beautiful idea must be the real idea, the idea that counts. It is doubtless best to compare it to a personality, to what in everyday life we call a character. Just as there exist beings who at first strike us with a semblance of originality and whose insignificance is revealed only over a long period, so there are ideas that deceive us. Nothing in this regard is more capable of leading into error than the striking novelty of a rhythm. In theory, then, it seems correct to say that the value of an idea can be tested only over a long period. One must live with it in order to know what it is and even *if* it is. In a moment we will attempt to explore what this may mean. First of all, let us note that such an idea can elicit from us a sudden fellow-feeling [*sympathie*] as in the case of the stranger that we meet for the first time and, unbeknown to us, is going to disappoint us. This is true of the most beautiful themes of César Franck; and we will have to ask ourselves how this is possible.

What does it mean then to live with an idea in such a way as to be able gradually to *experience* [*éprouver*] its reality, what we have called its "power of affirmation"? Here again it seems we must have recourse to the comparison we were making just now between an idea and a person. And yet a prejudicial objectivity at once comes into play. A person is not finished once and for all as is a musical idea; on the contrary, the person becomes; and the very way in which he becomes tends to determine our final judgment. It seems that, at the heart of this objection, however sensible it may appear, there is a failure to distinguish. When we say of a person that it would be necessary to live with him in order to judge him, we are completely abstracting from his possible transformations. Implicitly one can even say that we are denying them. We observe only that he is revealed to us progressively, which presupposes precisely that we treat him as really given once and for all. Shall we claim that, all the same, his way of behaving in successive situations instructs us and alone can help us to grasp what he is in his permanent and real unity, whereas the musical idea does not possess this ability to react in a different way in varying circumstances and that consequently there is no reason why it should reveal itself to us over a period of time? If things were thus we could at best hope to habituate ourselves, to adapt ourselves to the musical idea which *installs* itself in us definitively. But experience and reflection agree in showing that this interpretation is impossible. The idea that installs itself purely and simply is without doubt the idea that dies. In reality the power of affirmation of which we spoke at the beginning, that is to say, the life of the idea, consists precisely its ability to renew itself and at the same time to reveal itself little by little. Shall we say that this is at bottom an illusion—that it is we who are transformed and who renew it, who project onto it our changing reality? The objection has, I believe, scarcely any significance. For if it is correct to say that we put into the idea more and more of ourselves, it is nonetheless legitimate to affirm that we incorporate it into ourselves more and more intimately. The life of the idea is made up of this duality, of this invisible movement that only an exterior and faulty analysis can claim to decompose. The real, the living idea is the one that, when it has completed its work, does not leave us as it found us. There is no reason to choose between an interpretation according to which we have caused something of our own life to pass into it and an interpretation which says that the idea itself has enriched us. Once again, these are only two abstract ways of understanding one and the same process. No doubt it will be best to attribute to the living idea a power of suggestion reaching deeper and deeper levels within ourselves and to recognize that it participates, on the other hand, more and more completely in this rebirth that has already begun [*renaissance antérieure*], that it is more and more involved in this sort of individual *revival* that it has itself inspired. Doubtless the same is true of the person with whom we come to feel a deeper and deeper connection. In revealing himself to us he reveals us to ourselves. He helps us to recognize that we are richer than we thought and at the same time we are well aware that, far from just being the occasion for it, he contributes in fact to this unexpected unfolding. Between him and us, in reality, an indivisible "current" is established. We cannot hope to discern what is his share and what is ours in this spiritual community; and this is precisely what constitutes the charm of our exchange.

How does it come about that, having begun from the idea of authority, we are now heading for the milder climes of fellow-feeling? The contradiction between the two ideas is, I think, only apparent. To be sure, there is a brutal authority that subjugates but has no other hold on us. Here as everywhere else, it is life alone that decides. Sometimes a brutal person may become milder with time; but most often the soul does not forgive having first been taken by force. I am thinking of certain musical ideas of Beethoven, the crude strength of which we will never get used to. There are indiscreet ways of imposing oneself that are no more tolerable in an idea than in a person.

One may object that all this is very subjective, that one person adapts where another always balks, and that one could never find in so subjective a realm a criterion for the value of a musical idea. But few notions seem to me more equivocal than that of criterion. If one means by that a principle of determination capable of being valid for everyone, that is to say for any person whatsoever, we must state with the utmost insistence that there cannot be any criterion in such a matter. But can one conclude from that to the real equivalence of all musical ideas? If one stays with what the verb 'to please' ['*plaire*'] implies, I think that one must answer "Yes" without hesitation. It is incontestable that absolutely any work is always capable of pleasing someone. This can be presupposed before any inquiry, before any psycho-physiological investigation. But we have already said how much this word 'please' seems inadequate to us. What pleases pleases only in the instant. There is no life there, consequently no enrichment. The complex experience that we have tried to define is of a much more elevated order, and we must add that it can be had only by a relatively small number of privileged persons (who alone can claim to be musicians).

We thus arrive at this conclusion, still too simple and summary, that there is a hierarchy of "ideas" which can be defined only in connection with a hierarchy of spiritual lives.[2] Someone may object that a saint can have terrible musical taste and find in a weak or even ugly "idea" a beauty that an "expert" will deny to it. But we must be more specific here. His preference for Puccini, or for Massenet,[3] can have no significance whatsoever for his sanctity. It is even difficult to see, without further analysis, how a musical idea that he relishes in the same way that one enjoys an ice cream cone can contribute to nourishing his "sanctity"! The musical phrase pleases him.[4] The phrase pleases him, that's all. And this word 'please' must be understood here in its most immediate and consequently least spiritual meaning. Hence it is not on the level on which he is really superior that the idea lives in him, it does not contribute in any way to that superiority. In short, the one who enjoys the phrase in question is only nominally identical to the one who deserves our admiration.

Perhaps you will insist and ask if a musical idea truly needs to be beautiful in order to sustain, for example, the fervor of a believer, we could even say in order to feed his ardor and his zeal. No doubt music can have a stimulating value that is independent of its properly aesthetic quality. But note that we are here talking about something quite different. This stimulating or consoling virtue exhausts itself in the present; it does not survive the present. Now, what we are here concerned with is, on the contrary, the idea that remains for the mind and *develops* in it at the same time so that, under the influence of the idea, the mind deepens itself. And there can be no question of attributing a specifically moral action to the idea, which would be absurd and, from an aesthetic point of view, monstrous. The more and more intimate mutual relations that are established between us and the person with whom we have some fellow feeling are without any doubt extra-moral; but they enrich us, they make us more complete, more sensitive [*frémissant*]. They tend to blur the overly sharp edges of our nature, those limits that the spirit in us tolerates only with impatience. That is the inestimable service that the true musical idea provides us. Which readily explains why the profound idea should rarely be accessible on the first encounter, or at least why it is never absolutely accessible. The idea that we grasp immediately is the one which we are already capable of assimilating. It has no distance to travel in us; we can expect nothing from it. We can hope for nothing especially valuable from this overly friendly visitor. The idea that encounters resistance is sometimes one most likely to survive. But once again in all of this domain it is impossible to generalize. And it would be eminently dangerous to maintain *a priori* that the idea that strikes us at the outset is an idea without personality. It seems to us that it is in reality in the notion of promise that one can find the solution to the kind of antinomy we have just pointed out, the idea whose content unfolds itself immediately to our eyes like a flower with its corolla too widely opened is very close to dying. And there is a way of understanding that amounts to a condemnation. But in order to realize that the idea *gives* itself less than it *promises* itself, it is sufficient to remember that the connection between the idea and the one who grasps it is in reality a relation of being to being. Here, as in the strictly personal order, the possible, what one hopes for, plays

an essential role. To love a being is to give him credit, that is, to be
attached to him at least as much for what he will be as for what he
is. The intimate union of knowledge and mystery is, as it were, the
intellectual side of love. And in the same way, to understand an aes-
thetically beautiful idea here is to anticipate the future; it is to become
intoxicated in advance with all that we will owe to it. Only one needs,
I think, a broad experience of music to recognize immediately, in the
satisfaction that the new idea engenders in us, what the chances are, so
to say, that it will live; in order to appreciate what its power of spiritual
penetration may turn out to be.[5] A priori such an evaluation can even
seem impossible. And yet there is no doubt, as we have already said,
that there are ideas that at once create confidence in themselves and
whose instantaneous power of seduction, we affirm without hesitation,
scarcely hints at their profound vitality. Amongst these ideas the most
beautiful themes of César Franck figure in the first rank. And perhaps it
would be no more reasonable to ask about the sources of this precious
privilege than to wonder why such an innocent and deep childlike
gaze moves us to tears. In this order, as in all those in which the mind
tends to grasp itself outside of the infinite mediation of the temporal
data, the problem of origins and causes tends to lose more and more
its importance and even its significance.[6] No historical consideration
of whatever kind allows us to account for the beauty of a musical
idea (neither do the individual gifts of the person who discovered it).
We would of course uselessly push the problem back if we say that
the idea is limited to expressing in a particularly adequate way the
emotion felt by the musician. For we would still need to ask ourselves
how the musician had the ability to translate it with this rigor and, if
we answer that the emotion itself is unique, how it was given to him
to be the only one to feel it. Hence we consider that a musical idea,
such as the generating theme of the *Quartet in D*, is a miracle in the
most authentic sense of the term; moreover, whatever gropings may
have preceded it in Franck's work, any attempt to recognize in it the
pure and simple expression of a psycho-physiological nature probably implies a begging of the question and, in any case, an entirely
illegitimate use of certain categories, such as that of cause.

It remains for us to specify, through the study of specific examples from Franck's work, the still too general considerations that we have just discussed.

In any case, it goes without saying, the real musical idea cannot be reduced to a combination of signs, if only because it is always oriented, because it has a meaning/direction [*sens*]. This meaning is as definite, as characteristic as an disposition. We might even say that it is the dynamic equivalent of an disposition. There are ideas that leave, that depart (I am thinking, for example, of the theme of the Bach cantata *Mit Frieden und Freude fahr' ich dahin*); and, on the contrary, there are ideas that come toward us. Thus the theme that emerges in the middle of Franc's *Chorale in A* very clearly comes down to meet us. "Comes down to meet us," such is the dynamic content of this theme. It is obvious that one could be more precise, but in any case the idea is actively turned towards us. It is as if it raises us to itself in a sublime and spontaneous impulse of generosity. No doubt it does not exhaust itself in the gift it makes of itself to us. It seems obliged to re-possess itself again and, as it were, to climb back into itself. But it returns to itself only after a final gesture or a final pitying look in our direction. It comes to an end on one of those pitying and doleful inflections that are so characteristic of Franck's musical ideas in general. Even the dominant phrase, the phrase that is maintained throughout, never seems in Franck to be absolutely sufficient to itself. It is as though it quivers with a sort of secret longing; it is as though the thought of souls to be saved haunts and disturbs its blessedness. If Franck, alone perhaps since Johann-Sebastian Bach, has been able to express the divine directly, it is because he has found the means of rendering with an unheard of intensity the anxious solicitude with which the divine thought is turned towards men: the ineffable mystery of the communication between the human and the divine is at the very heart of his music. And this is intimately linked to the revealing power properly speaking, to this capacity the idea has in itself to cause fellow feeling and faith to flow into us immediately. We must be more precise. It can happen, as we have already said, that the idea is the imperious act of affirmation of a masculine will that wants to tame us: for example, the initial theme of Beethoven's Fifth Symphony. It can also happen that it at once expresses, like certain phrases of Schumann, the human anguish of a heart that no longer belongs to itself and suffers from waiting and being dependent. Franck's typical musical idea is of a completely different order. Most often it develops broadly, sometimes it even unfolds like a great spiritual corolla. In any case, nothing is easier and nobler than this very smooth development, for which one could find analogies only in the cantatas and passions of Bach and in a few rare adagios of Beethoven. Even at that, in Beethoven the pathos of inspiration is never surmounted as completely as in Franck. To be sure, Beethoven's typical idea is always the answer of man to man, an expression, sublime to be sure, of resolution and resignation; but not the fervent Annunciation of another order. With Franck it is really as though the idea always has a mediating function. It is sometimes a grace; it can also be an intercession. But always it seems poised between two worlds, the fundamental duality which Beethoven was not able to recognize. I think the completely general reflections that I have exposed in the first part of this study will allow us to glimpse how the idea can possess this power of interior renewal and of reconciliation.

The American philosopher Hocking has observed that the properly religious quality of a soul is doubtless the one that can be recognized the most immediately, precisely because it affects the whole person and not this or that particular fragment of the person. He adds that the person is infallibly revealed through a radical originality in its way of appreciating, at the same time as through a kind of spontaneous belief in its own infallibility in spiritual matters that one must be careful not to confuse with presumptuousness. (The true believer has a share in eternity; he knows it; he judges all things from the point of view of eternity.) We think that these characteristics can be admirably applied to Franck's musical idea conceived of as a person. It is at once obvious indeed that this idea is a belief; that is, rather than positing itself with its own dynamic power, it affirms another order with which it communicates and whose brightness it reflects to us insofar as it is able. I do not know any idea less infatuated with itself, that is to say, that claims less omnipotence for itself. A sort of ineradicable timidity is joined in it to the highest certitude. It is filled for us with divine seedings [*semences*] and it is as though it trembles at the idea of losing any of it. That is what we meant when we said that it is mediating. One could, I think, define much more precisely Franck's musical idea through a patient analysis of its structure. The very striking role played by half-tone intervals in Franck's music seems to us particularly revealing here. One recognizes in it, as it were, the concern to follow the precise contours of an experience of suffering, instead of simply giving a vague and stylized reproduction of it. "Closer to thee, ever closer": this is what these ardent and chaste phrases seem to say to us. Between our mourning or our uncertainty and their power of revelation, a mystical exchange seems to establish itself. The idea grows tender and becomes human, and the soul touched by it finds once again the strength it was lacking. To help live; to help bring things to life: such is the sacred function of a music like that of César Franck. And, without a doubt, it is thereby that it has been able to have a marvelous influence on our entire school. It would scarcely be an exaggeration to say that contemporary French music came out of Franck's music, as once all secular music came from church music and popular song. I think that this influence of Franck cannot be overestimated and that it has been infinitely more profound, more inward than that of the Wagnerians (amongst whom works of the first order can be seen in Chausson's *Symphonie, le Chant de la Cloche* and *Fervaal*, but not much else). The extent and degree of this influence can be understood all the better because Franck's music, in spite of what one might have been tempted to infer from the preceding characterization, is not, properly speaking, specialized. There is a typical color Franck gives to all the emotions, to joy as to suffering and longing. Think, for example, of the Allegro of the Sonata for piano and violin, one of his most moving creations, much superior, in my opinion, to the Introduction, of which the melancholy, perhaps a bit factitious, recalls certain compositions of Eduard Grieg, and superior to the Finale which borders on vulgarity in a few places.[7] The Allegro is alive with an extraordinary pathos; it initially recalls certain works of Schumann. Nevertheless its inspiration is different. Compare this Allegro, for example, to the pathos of the introduction of the *Sonata in A Minor* for piano and violin which has some similarity to it. Schumann's musical idea seems to take a sort of romantic pleasure in its own destruction; it abandons itself happily to the whirlwind that carries it off, and seems to have no other aspiration than to be dispersed at the whim of the hurricane. In contrast, Franck's musical idea tends, with the most pathetic ardor, towards deliverance, towards its consummation. It evokes in us a kind of fervent pity, and the spiritual theme that it awakens in our hearts is manifested musically by means of a second idea, a phrase of consolation that calms the sobbings of the first. Franck's music seems to us, in short, to be redolent of a tenderness that is more serious, more masculine than that of Schumann whose effusions end by tiring us. One sometimes has the feeling that Schumann would simply not know how to proceed if he did not have the sufferings of his heart to confide to us.[8] But Franck does not have this rather indiscreet impetuosity which makes the listener recoil a bit. He is not of the sort who, less out of sincerity than out of the need, really a little indecent or puerile, to keep nothing for himself, bares his soul completely. Puerile, I have said, for there is inexperience in this lack of restraint. Franck's discretion is, to my mind, one of his most singular merits. His art is not bloodless, it is pure. And the one has nothing to do with the other. We feel sorry for the person who does not sense the infinite interior richness of *Psyche* or the *Quartet in D*. But just what is this purity that is the complete contrary of having everything stripped away? And how is it that it never makes us sad or never disappoints us as does something that is lacking? This is because Franck's melodies seem most often to conceal an intimate and painful secret; only, is this secret really its own? Is it not rather ours? We will have to wonder about this. Think, for example, of the Andante of the *Quintet*—infinitely more beautiful, in my opinion, than that of the *Symphony* in which the strings respond with so tragic a refusal to the more and more urgent, more and more passionate appeals of the piano. What gravity there is in this decision to be silent! Nothing is less similar to the manner of playing hide-and-go-seek with oneself that is so irritating in certain followers of Debussy. And this is why this song of a perfect candor has nevertheless for us the immediate pathos of an allusion or a memory. Is it remorse or, on the contrary, longing that it renews in us? How can one decide? In any case, it scarcely matters. But in my opinion here is what *is* essential. A work such as *Parsifal*, which is a hymn to purity, is not and cannot be a pure work, for the pure do not recognize themselves as such, and purity could never celebrate itself without transforming into its opposite.[9] Wagner continuously *points out* Parsifal to us, and this music that bears all the passions and all intoxications resembles some gigantic *Ecce homo*. "He now, he is pure; he—he alone." It is the sinner in us, it is Amfortas who is moved before the supernatural innocence of the Saint. Franck's music, in contrast, precisely because it *thinks with purity*, seems to turn its half-closed eyes towards the dangerous wounds draining us of our life's blood. It prefers, no doubt, not to know. But it guesses at them and it pardons us for them. Its innocent heart comes to beat next to ours. Its fraternal hands are placed gently on our brow. It is as though it had been given a mission and as though, in order for it to be accomplished, we agree to hand over to it our palpitating and rebellious soul. Here perhaps is why Franck has so rarely been able to express joy without falling into clumsiness and vulgarity, without redundant and mechanical formulas in place of the suppleness of a truly sincere and moving inspiration. Franck's musical idea in its truth is always a distinct person—a Mediator we have said, with whom our soul concludes an alliance, an original and carefully nuanced pact. Hence in general Franck is not capable of carrying us away in a cosmic whirlwind like Beethoven or Wagner, our own rhythm allowing itself to be submerged in the universal rhythm. But this is precisely the way in which musical thought in Franck is essentially mystical. Contrary to the claims of a rationalism that assimilates religion only on condition of annihilating it, the absorption of the individual into the anonymous totality of the Absolute Spirit can probably not satisfy the soul of a believer. There is no true salvation except when a dialogue is engaged between the human person and the divine person, when there is a Savior Who receives the glorified creature into His embrace. It was given to César Franck, and to him alone after Johann-Sebastian Bach, to suggest, at least, what this singular experience can be to the very persons who have no concepts to which they can relate it and who consequently believe they must reject it with all the force of their reason. The most illustrious of César Franck's disciples, M. Vincent d'Indy, in whom the spark has remained alive, was to have the glorious mission of deepening what in Franck remains entirely unexpressed, that is, to make concrete this mystical union of nature and charity realized for the believer in miracles and in conversion.[10]

Notes

[1] This article originally appeared in *La Civilisation française*, November, 1920.

[2] We should note that this hierarchy can exist in each one of us taken individually.

[3] *Translator's note*: Both Puccini and Massenet wrote operas based upon the Abbé Prévost's *Manon Lescaut*.

[4] We see no reason to deny that there can be an art of pleasing the ear that includes formulas in the same way as is true for the art of pleasing the palate. There is here a technique which would be of interest to and doubtless instructive for the psycho-physiologist [*psychophysician*]. It goes without saying that it has nothing to do with aesthetics as such.

[5] One sees without difficulty that there must be an intimate correspondence between what we have agreed to call the development of the idea and this life in us to which the idea is called. The development is essentially only the first step of this intimate becoming by which the idea is called to become more and more our own; it is like the first tracing of a path which subsequently will become more and more enmeshed in the inward regions of the individual soul.

[6] In this way the principally negative value of the idea of creation is defined. Creation exists wherever the causal explanation, always possible in theory, turns out to be insignificant, wherever it remains really exterior to what one needs to reduce and what is really irreducible.

[7] This will become obvious if you compare it to the Finale of the Quintet of Fauré, rather similar in inspiration, but with a delicacy, a winged grace in joy that one does not find in the Finale in question.

[8] It is precisely where he is the most sober that he is the most deeply moving. Think, for example, of melodies such as *Le Noyer* or *Au Loin* or of the sublime introduction of the Andante in the *Trio in D Minor*.

[9] Or at least without appearing to parody itself. Think, for example, of certain passages of Gounod, or even the worst parts of *Redemption*.

[10] Fifteen years later Marcel returned to the "musical idea" in a critique that it seems interesting to put here: "Reflections on an operetta: *Vacances*" by Duvernois, André Barde, and Maurice Yvain. "I do not know if the place occupied in our society by the culture of obsession has been made sufficiently clear. It is from this perspective that one must consider, even outside of publicity in all its forms, the bouncy [*trepidante*] operetta of the last few years and also, I believe, the cinema itself.

What is the inward significance of this general fact? One could write a lot about this. What strikes me above all is that it is essentially a phenomenon of despair or, what comes to the same thing, the consequence of what one could call the general collapse of the interior life. Domestic obsessions take the place of thought. They fill out our lives and at the same time they create a sort of pseudo-cheeriness in which one must believe many people today are fooled.

What appears serious to me is that there exists today a collusion between this technique of auditory obsession and the music of the musicians. And this could happen only insofar as music itself has betrayed its essential mission, insofar as it has denied soul itself, of which it had been the privileged mode of expression. It will be necessary, I think, to consider the history of music in the course of the last few years in the light of this denial. And one will no doubt notice that, among the most illustrious, an increasing number of composers have lost the sense of what must normally be the life of a musical idea and its development within a fervent thought nourished by it, and that they have tended to reduce it to its caricature or even to its opposite: a blind obsession, a demoniacal possession." (*1935*, January, 1935)

Bergson and Music[1]

Nothing, as it were, is more contrary to the spirit of M. Bergson's philosophy than to ask a question like the one we will pose here; and this is so for several connected reasons.

In the first place, no doubt there is no idea less Bergsonian than that of Bergsonism. Indeed, the intimate tragedy of this difficult and powerful thought is its incapacity, on the basis of its very premises, ever to be converted into a system—or, if you will, to complete itself without at the same time denying itself. How, insofar as it is itself a superior mode of the life of the spirit, would it not also bear the seal of the unpredictable or of perpetual creation, and would it not be consequently condemned—or consecrated [*vouée*]—to remaining ever open, far from ever "completing itself" like fitting the keystone in a Gothic arch? There can thus be no question of deriving this or that corollary supposedly bearing on music from a certain body of propositions called Bergsonism

The idea of a theory of music, of the very possibility of such a theory, scarcely seems to me capable of finding a meaning in a philosophy that was always concerned to maintain, as strongly as Aristotle or Comte, the absolute distinctness of the various spiritual domains or, if you will, the modes of experience, and that views uneasily and suspiciously the attempts to rationalize these modes, to substitute abstract equivalents for them. It is entirely in keeping with all we know about M. Bergson to admit that for him, if a philosophy of music is possible, this can only be at the end of a long inquiry of the same kind, in sum, as the one to which, after having treated experimental psychology, he once submitted biology. In other words, it would be a grave mistake to think that the writings M. Bergson has published until now can by themselves justify in his eyes any claim regarding the nature of musical inspiration or of the special universe it reveals to us. Even at that, we must recognize that such an inquiry could not possibly consist of a simple conscientious collection of facts, of information about the psychology of the musician or about his technique. It should be entirely suffused by the vital breath that inspires not only M. Bergson's books [taken individually] but also his thought [in general] considered at once in its aesthetic and personal unity. This is to say that essentially he alone would be capable of pursuing this inquiry; and *he will not do it*. Other tasks, more essential in his eyes, call for his attention and will occupy him in the years he can still consecrate to philosophical speculation. No doubt it has often pleased M. Bergson to say that he was making only a partial contribution to a great collective work that others would pursue after him. The time has come, he seems to be saying, for philosophy to give up overly ambitious syntheses and to be content with limited results that would organize themselves little by little—moreover, in a way unforseeable by the very ones who uncovered them. If things were really thus, we could hope that some day a successor to M. Bergson will bring us this philosophy of music that the author of *Matière et mémoire*[2] has not given us, but that would continue his psychology. Unfortunately, it is greatly to be feared lest this optimistic and social view of the speculative enterprise should be in great part illusory. Perhaps it is even in contradiction with the doctrine of philosophical intuition that M. Bergson expounded, notably at the Bologna Conference. Nobody can have any confidence in the "disciples" of M. Bergson, no doubt he himself least of all. If they are not simply commentators, they will be virtuosi who perform dangerous variations on themes whose solidity or precise power of development they can in no way be sure of being able to evaluate.

All these preliminary remarks may seem otiose. I consider them indispensable for limiting in the strictest fashion the importance of the reflections that follow.

In reality, it is extremely difficult for a reader of M. Bergson not to suppose—wrongly, moreover—that a certain philosophy of music is implicit in the theory of concrete duration [*la durée concrète*]. And perhaps we have the right in these conditions—without deluding ourselves about the ultimate value of this inquiry—to apply ourselves to elucidating this very philosophy and to see in what measure it is in agreement with direct experience.

* * *

To begin with, it seems difficult to admit that it is by pure chance that M. Bergson has used, as regularly as he does, the image of a melody in order to make concrete what he means by *la durée pure*. Let us reread in particular the famous passage of *Essai sur les données immédiates de la conscience*.[3]

> Absolutely pure duration is the form taken by the succession of our conscious states when our self allows itself to live, when it abstains from establishing a separation between the present state and the previous states. In order to do so it does not need to absorb itself completely in the sensation of the passing idea, for then, on the contrary, it would cease to endure. Nor does it need to forget the previous states. It suffices that in recalling these states, it does not juxtapose them to the current state, like a point to another point, but organizes them with it, as it happens when we recall the notes of a melody, *fused together as it were*. Could one not say that, even if these notes follow upon one another, we *perceive* them nevertheless in each other and that their totality is comparable to a living being whose parts, although distinct, penetrate each other as the direct result of their solidarity? The proof of this is that, if we break the measure by unreasonably emphasizing one note of the melody, it is not its exaggerated length as such that will alert us to our fault, but the qualitative change brought to the musical phrase as a whole. (*loc. cit.*, pp. 75-7)

It is certain that, when one reads a passage like the one I have just quoted (and that is far from being the only one in M. Bergson's works), one is tempted to wonder if a certain experience of music, reflected upon, is not in some way at the basis of the doctrine, does not *underlie* it, so to speak. Here too, however, the strictest prudence is necessary. Is it not simply to avoid any confusion that M. Bergson has recourse to this musical comparison, and could he not essentially just as well have used, by way of example, a *spoken* phrase in which the words and the silences that separate them likewise organize themselves in such a way as to form an indivisible whole? For my part, I am entirely convinced of it. The *durée concrète* is not musical in its essence. At most one can say—using, moreover, a language of which, no doubt and rightly, M. Bergson would not approve—that melodic continuity provides us with an example, an illustration of a pure continuity, which is the job of the philosopher to apprehend in itself, in its reality at once universal and concrete.

However, this general observation does not dispense us from asking how far the theory of duration, as it is presented in the *Essai* for example, contributes to clarifying the nature of what I hope I may call the musical phenomenon [*le fait musical*]. A preliminary distinction, moreover, imposes itself here. It does not seem that the doctrine of the *Essai* can give us any direct enlightenment about the *elementary musical values*. It scarcely allows us to understand how it can be that sound is accompanied by an irreducible emotional indicator. And the following sentence does not help us to clarify the difficulty. M. Bergson asks,

> Would one understand the expressive power of music if one did not admit that we repeat interiorly the sounds heard in such a way as to place ourselves back in the psychological state from which they issued, an original state that one could not possibly express but that the movements adopted by the entirety of our body suggest to us? (p. 33)

I would not dream of denying that there is truth here. But it is perhaps dangerous to suppose, as M. Bergson seems to do here, that the sound emanates, strictly speaking, from a psychological state, to which it allows us to return by a sort of recoil [*choc en retour*].

In contrast, it is noticeably more instructive when the *Essai* deals with the musical idea or, if you prefer, the melody strictly speaking. Let us leave aside the perhaps slightly inappropriate words that I thought it necessary to emphasize in the first quotation.[4] An analysis like the one that M. Bergson attempts incontestably highlights—or at least helps us to define—the wholly unusual type of unity we find in a melody. It is a unity at once undivided and fluid, a unity of a process and not of a thing. Perhaps, however, without my daring to state it absolutely, the complex reality of the musical experience in a way exceeds the description that M. Bergson gives of it. Here I can do nothing but refer only very briefly to a very important point. What happens precisely when I *follow* the development of a melody? Is it completely sufficient to say that the notes of a melody penetrate each other and are organized amongst themselves? M. Bergson speaks of "the successive notes of a melody by which we allow ourselves to be lulled" (*loc. cit.* p. 78). And this helps us to understand how he imagined—or rather how he refuses to imagine—musical becoming. In the final analysis it seems that for him listening to a melody is a way of dreaming it, that it is what a German would perhaps call *hineinträumen* [literally, "dreaming into"], an almost unlimited state of relaxation, a pure interior flowing. And according to him this way of experiencing the melody, of becoming the melody, is doubtless entirely different from the act by which it is represented or imagined as a line—that is to say, spatialized. But I am not sure that this absolute opposition between the melody as experienced and the melody as imagined is not too strong. Following the musical phrase is not only passing unawares from note to note. It is at the same time, at least to some degree, dominating this passage. And M. Bergson certainly admits it. But is not this act by which I dominate it—which is in no degree a mode of conception or intellection—the act by which what is in fact flowing becomes consciousness of this flowing and, in some way at least, representation, figuration—but non- spatial—of becoming?

When we speak of the beauty of a melodic line, the aesthetic characterization does not involve the interior process, but a certain object, a certain figure—non-spatial, I repeat, or at any rate, a figure of which the world of extension could only give us inadequate symbolizations. This would surely require extensive clarifications. I am well aware how shocking the idea of a non-spatial figure is for the intellect. But we would have to know if, to give an account of musical experience, we are nevertheless not obliged to introduce a notion of this type. As I pass from note to note, a certain whole is constructed, a form builds itself that surely cannot be reduced to an organized succession of states, any more than an object is distinguishable from the sensory modifications that its presence causes in the subject. Doubtless it is of the essence of this form to be given only in *la durée*; but it itself transcends in some fashion the purely temporal mode according to which it manifests itself. From this point of view it is relatively easy to perceive what one generally means by musical comprehension. Is it not identical in fact to the act by which the form constructs itself? Is it not the case that failure to understand is precisely to remain at the stage in which the states follow upon one another, even interpenetrate each other if you like, but without subordinating themselves to *a real musical being*? Unless one admits that incomprehension consists in the successive sounds not even becoming organized amongst themselves but remaining, on the contrary, discontinuous. This would then be only the total failure of memory for a consciousness incapable of going beyond the purely instantaneous. Rightly or wrongly, I tend to think that such is the interpretation that M. Bergson would be inclined to give of a fact that is as common as it is poorly defined.

However, does he properly account for what experience reveals to us? One can doubt it. Each of us has had these moments of interior illumination when a phrase that one was following, but without recognizing its internal necessity, suddenly reveals itself to be in harmony with its mysterious essence. But this act of apperception, the equivalent of which it would not be difficult to find in the religious or mystical order, cannot in any way be reduced to the sympathy that allows me to wed the phrase, to live it. I would be inclined to say that it is not a letting go, but, on the contrary, a kind of mastery. Are we talking here about what M. Bergson calls intuition? It is possible; but nothing is, to tell the truth, less certain. Is it not the defining characteristic of intuition, in fact, to bear upon what happens, on the creative process at its source? Now, is not the revelation in question here rather the discovery of an order that is doubtless not abstractly *conceived* but one that, nevertheless, one can also not, strictly speaking, call *given*. Everything happens as if we were abruptly associated with the will of the musician, as though this will, having become our own, found in the idea its only satisfaction. Just as philosophical solutions, far from having an intrinsic significance, remain relative to a certain way of conceiving the problems—so here the musical order is a *completion*; it does not impose itself on us right away except on condition of *answering an expectation in some fashion* .

The music that I do not understand is, taking these words rigorously, the kind that does not correspond to anything in me. And is it not clear that *here* we are arriving on a shore where the thought of M. Bergson is ready to receive us. It seems to me that the musician asks me to place myself on a certain spiritual level from which it is possible for me to *join* him. With regard to attentive recognition, "It is necessary," says M. Bergson, "that the listener should place himself at the outset among the corresponding ideas and should develop them into auditory representations corresponding to the brute sounds by following a rhythmic pattern [*schéma moteur*]." (*Matière et mémoire*, p. 112) I think this can be applied here with a minimum of transposition. A person who does not grasp a musical development is in a position analogous to a person before whom one speaks an unknown language. The preconditions are not present that would permit him to disarticulate appropriately and to reorganize the indistinct whole that is immediately given to him. Only, of course, it is not strictly speaking memories corresponding to the sounds that must be recovered here. But let us remember that for M. Bergson memory is in no way that faded reproduction of perception to which associationist psychology tries to reduce it. The author of *Matière et mémoire* ceaselessly puts us on guard against such an interpretation, which implies in his eyes the most radical misunderstanding of the spiritual life. Memory and perception are entirely heterogeneous with regard to one another. And I wonder if one would distort the thought of M. Bergson in maintaining that a pure memory, that is to say, entirely removed from the actualizing influence of the body, is by its very essence ungraspable. I do not think that we can in any way imagine pure memory. We can only conceive of it as a limit placed beyond, or more exactly, on the hither side of the representable.

Consequently it would not be absurd, it seems to me, to claim that the musician appeals to *memories* in us that alone enable us, let us not say to *understand* him, but to *hear* him. And one could show that any authentic musical creation consists first of all in conjuring up in us *a certain past*. This seems to me no less clear for Mozart than for Schumann, for Wagner than for Debussy. Perhaps we would not be entirely misled by a metaphor in saying that the musician of genius is like a prism through which the anonymous and neutral—optically neutral—Past that forms the depth of each one of us decomposes itself, becomes specified, and colors itself with individual nuances: a temporal prism. I am well aware of the not only paradoxical but also overly sophisticated appearance that such a way of conceiving musical originality inevitably takes on. But this is due precisely to the fact that we are for the most part very far from having yet assimilated the most original elements of M. Bergson's doctrine.

When I speak of the decomposition of the past, it is very difficult not to think that for me it involves subdividing the past into historical slices. Mozart would take me back to Vienna in the eighteenth century, Monteverdi to Mantua a century and a half or two centuries earlier, etc. Moreover, it would be through a play of the association of infinitely diversified ideas that this type of evocation would take place. But here no such thing is actually involved. Here the past is not this or that portion of an historical becoming that is more or less explicitly assimilated to a movement in space, to a cinematic succession. It is essentially inexplicable in itself, in relationship to which the present not only orders itself, but even more and especially characterizes itself. These multiple pasts are fundamentally lived perspectives [*perspectives sentimentales*] according to which our life can be relived, not insofar as it is a series of events, but to the extent that it is an indivisible unity that art alone allows us to apprehend as such—art or love, perhaps.

It goes without saying that there are types of music that this scheme fits much less well than others. A Stravinsky, far from resembling conjurers like Debussy or Fauré for example, seems on the contrary to take on the task, so to say, of isolating us from our past, of introducing us into a *re-inforced present*, a cosmic present I dare say, in that the personality is annihilated.

In my opinion things are absolutely different, in spite of the misleading appearances, for a Wagner who prolongs our memory into a theogony and reestablishes a continuity between individual duration and the duration of the universe. One could show, I think, that the art of Stravinsky, through the way in which it abolishes any distinction between the superficial and the profound in sheer dynamic, is absolutely opposed to a philosophy for which being can be grasped as degrees of intensity, or more exactly, interiority hierarchized by the effort, itself graduated, of a consciousness actively at work on itself. The world of Stravinsky is foreign to consciousness. I am for my part strongly tempted to think that it is *on the hither side* of consciousness.

And it is only for this reason that one can speak in its regard with M. de Schloezer of "objective music."

Perhaps these indications, properly developed, would allow us to elucidate in some fashion what we mean by a profound musical idea. The profound idea presents itself to us, I think, with a twofold character. On the one hand, it seems to come *from afar*, on the other hand, it corresponds to the relaxing of an effort, to what I would like to call a *relaxation coming from on high*. I am convinced that if we succeeded in analyzing these two aspects of the profound idea we would manage to attain essential truths. First of all it is quite remarkable—and I begin with the second point—that the concentration of the will in no wise suffices to give us the feeling of this new dimension that we are calling 'depth'. Works such as d'Indy's *String Quartets*, in which this concentration is pushed to the extreme, are in this regard very significant. Here when the relaxation comes about, it is always in the direction [*sens*] of development, that is to say, of a mechanism. With the greatest composers, on the contrary (and I am thinking of Beethoven's last quartets as well as of Fauré's quintets), one would say that this relaxation comes about in an opposite direction, and by paths that are ordinarily closed to the artist. This relaxation corresponds surely to what makes the profoundest idea at the same time the one that appears to me the most *natural*; only, here again, one must pay very close attention. For the word 'natural' can have opposite meanings. If today I hear a work by some faithful disciple of Debussy for example, everything in it appears *natural* to me in that everything comes to arrange itself straight off in certain established frameworks. This music not only does not in any way disturb my habits, but, even more, adapts itself to them spontaneously because it is itself the effect of imitation. But just now I was using the word 'natural' in a quite different sense. There is *non-surprise* from the moment there is *non-resistance*. But this non-resistance can very well not be due to the existence of habitual forms into which the proffered matter is poured. It can be due to the presence in me of an emptiness not yet experienced as such, of an active absence and of a sort of call exercised by this emptiness itself. This happens sometimes in love. This also happens, I think, in the greatest artistic achievements. And we find again the experience of fulfilled expectation that is at the heart of aesthetic intellection. In this sense, the profound idea is the one that strikes me where I am still vulnerable, where the hardening contracted under the influence of repetition, that is to say, the mechanization of myself, still has lacunae. In a word, it constructs me; it is *formative*.

What now is this distance that the idea seems to have traversed in me? Here we meet take up again what I have said just now about the function of the past in music. But I think we must add that the past from which the idea seems to spring has as its essential character that of being an *unutilized* past. And here Proust can, if not complete, at least illustrate Bergson's thought in the most valuable way. "At whatever moment that we consider it," says Proust, "our soul as a whole has only an almost fictive value, in spite of the extensive list of its riches." (*Sodome et Gomorrhe*, II, t. I, p. 178) The profound idea possesses the miraculous gift of putting an end to this *unavailability* [*indisponibilité*] of ourselves. It re-establishes between me and myself communications that I may have thought abolished. Contemporary psychology gives us some light here: I receive a letter that I open with the feeling of vague and, as it were, impersonal curiosity. But this letter brings me a serious piece of news that affects me. Everything happens as though it forced my self to come out, as though it *pushed* me out in the open. This emotion is like the discovery that "does involve me after all." In short, it recalls me to the awareness of my own existence. I think that what is happening here is of an altogether analogous order. The profound idea is the one that causes a sudden *re-memoration of myself*; but that does not imply, at least in principle, any representation of any past *event* whatsoever. It gives me immediate access to a level on which *I am with myself.* And if there is a possible foundation for a musical mysticism, it seems to me that this is it. But one sees at once how much a philosophy of pure quality like M. Bergson's helps to make understandable for us this progress in interiority, this journey-ing towards a spiritual nuptial whose possibility a metaphysics of the concept, in contrast, could not possibly allow us even to perceive.

Is there any need to add, moreover, that the indications that I have striven to give, and the insufficiency and obscurity of which I am well aware, could be clarified only through special studies of the musical inspiration of the great creators, each of these being considered as the bearer of a message without intellectual content, but that each time renews and reconciles the soul who deciphers it.

Notes

1. This originally appeared in *La Revue Musicale*, VI, no. 5 (March, 1925).
2. *Translator's note*: This appeared originally in 1896 and was translated into English by N. Paul and W. Palmer as *Matter and Memory* (London: George Allen and Unwin, 1911).
3. *Translator's note*: This appeared originally in 1889 and has been translated into English by F. Pogson as *Time and Free Will: An Essay on the Immediate Data of Consciousness* (New York: Macmillan, 1919).
4. He is referring here to *fondues pour ainsi dire ensemble* and to *apercevons*, which we have translated: "fused together as" and "perceived" respectively.

Music Understood and Music Experienced[1]

In a recent issue of *Mesures* M. Boris de Scholezer has published a remarkable article on "Music, a Misunderstood Art" ("*la musique, art méconnu*") that calls for extensive commentary. I would like to indicate here the points on which I agree with him and those, no less important, that appear to me such as to raise reasonable objections.

What is a musical work? asks the author. Consider, for example, the first Prelude in C of [Bach's] *Well Tempered Clavier*. It is first of all a page covered with signs representing a particular system of sounds. A person called the performer will have to intervene in order to effect the transformation from the graphic into the audile. He produces aural vibrations that reach me, the listener, and give birth in me to complex and multiple states of consciousness. Where is the work of the musician? There is no sense in saying that this work is the page marked with signs. That is only a sketch intended to fix the thought of the musician in a schematic form. But the work consists even less in the aural vibrations themselves. They vanish once their office of transmission has been accomplished. If we move on to the sensation, the situation is far from clarifying itself. The sensations of the composer himself have disappeared with him. Must one say then that the work is made up of sensations in *us*? But even the reality of this "us" is singularly precarious. Our sensations cannot be isolated from a certain affective context that is essentially variable. What touched me yesterday leaves me indifferent today. Moreover, how can one not take into account the mediation of the performer who has his own personality and who, moreover, not being a machine, also varies from day to day? It seems then that our prelude dissolves "into hundreds, into thousands of images without consistency that vanish almost as soon as they are born. Its existence seems to be reduced to perpetual metamorphoses." In all of this, where is the stable element, the kernel, as one might say? The composer has traced the outline of a device for arousing sensation and emotions. But what are these emotions? They seem to have to depend on both the listener and the interpreter to such an extent that it seems impossible to assign them a determinable nature.

   Proceeding along this path, we end up with the most relativistic and ruinous conclusions. There is only one way to escape this impasse, declared M. Boris de Schloezer: frankly to abandon subjectivism in all its forms, for they all end up with the negation of music. You must understand by that the negation of the specific reality of the musical work and recognize that there is in the musical work an element that can be reduced neither to what is written nor to the aural vibrations nor to the states of consciousness. This last expression is not very felicitous, or rather is not sufficiently precise. But the meaning is clear. The work must have a content proper to it. This content M. Boris de Schloezer declares, not without hastiness, cannot be emotional, otherwise one falls back into subjectivism and the expression is no longer anything more than an acoustic phenomenon. This content, this meaning must be of an intellectual order, and our task is to understand it. I will at once point out that the terms 'emotional' and 'intellectual' should be defined much more carefully and that they are very likely of a nature to mislead. The author at once adds, rightly, that if the content of a discourse can always be detached from the form it has taken, this is not true here. The meaning of the musical work cannot strictly speaking be detached from form. Meaning cannot be examined apart from form in abstraction from the series of sounds. But here too the analysis seems to me insufficient. Let us note that, even in the domain of speech, a meaning cannot be directly dissociated from the form. What is possible is to substitute for one expression another more directly graspable, through which the meaning will appear more distinctly than through the first. Manifestly this substitution is not practicable in the musical order. The expression forms a single body with the content expressed to the degree that the expression is perfect. Let us suppose now that the expression is, on the contrary, imperfect, insufficient. The situation will not be the same as in speech. It can happen that I have an idea and that I do not manage to communicate it. Nevertheless, it seems to me that this idea is in me. It really preexists the adequate expression I am looking for and that I have not found. In the musical order, things are not completely the same. I say, not completely. The thought comprehends itself only after it has found its expression. It is in this expression and by means of it that the thought constitutes itself for itself. All the same, it is very probable that between these two limit cases there is, as its were, a continuum, or at least an indefinite string of intermediaries. The farther one gets from the zone in which the idea is a plan for action, a collection of actions to accomplish, the more one penetrates into the non-pragmatizable—that is to say, essentially into metaphysics—the more the idea, I think, tends to approximate the melody that the composer intuits and around which he gives himself up to a multitude of attempts, of gropings meant to *release* it, in the way one frees a spring or a vein of gold. It is only too clear, moreover, that lyric poetry constitutes here an essential link between metaphysical thinking and musical thinking. M. De Schloezer realizes it, moreover, since he writes that music is like the limit, in the mathematical sense, of poetry and even of all the arts.

The act of listening to music, he says correctly, implies that the listener maintains the aural series intact in his consciousness. Here sound A does not lead us simply towards the following sound B; it itself takes on a new value, A-prime, in relation to this B which gives it its meaning. "I understand this series. I discover its meaning when I grasp its immanent unity. And, as a result, I find myself faced with a complex system of relationships that adhere to each other and interpenetrate each other, a system in which each sound and each group of sounds is situated within a whole, assumes a definite function and acquires a specific quality due to its multiple relations with the others."

There is here, I will say, an obvious truth, but one that, if it is not at once supplemented, is in danger of leading us towards a disastrous intellectualism. It is beyond doubt, on the one hand, that listening amounts to an effort to understand, and, on the other hand, that understanding is essentially recognizing a certain structure. I grant thus absolutely to M. de Schloezer that a musical phenomenalism that abstracts from the structure would allow the essential to escape. Much more, that it would be incapable of grasping anything at all of what here makes the work possible and constitutes it as such. Simply understanding is not in itself appreciating. I can recognize a structure, but without abandoning a total indifference to it. It is for me a certain object that I apprehend, something whose development I follow, but which *says nothing to me*. M. De Schloezer has such a phobia of what he calls 'psychologism', he takes so far the concern to purify the musical content of everything that confers on it the power to affect us, that he is quite simply in danger of ending up with a complete sterilization of this mysterious reality that he is attempting to grasp. Nothing for that matter seems to me more dangerous than to take his examples as he does from *The Well Tempered Clavier* or from *The Art of the Fugue*. Let us take Johann Sebastian Bach. I do not ask for anything better. But then it should be the complete Bach of the *Cantatas*, of the *Passions*, or, again, of particular works, of particular sonatas, particular concertos in which his lyricism blossoms completely. I assuredly do not mean that this lyricism does not persist in both *The Well Tempered Clavier* and in *The Art of the Fugue*. It is even this lyricism that vitalizes the purely formal, such that never, or almost never, does this formalism become "academic". But the temptation for a theoretician will always be to overturn here the true hierarchy of values and to claim that the emotion is linked to the very perfection of the formal arrangement. This is absurd—even, to my mind, the major heresy in this domain. If emotion is not at the very beginning, it will not be anywhere. "The work once as it is understood," writes M. De Schloezer, "is generative of feelings, emotions, diverse thoughts." Agreed, but why? Is it the understanding itself that is generative? Surely not. For the musician the work itself has been a certain way of living through an emotion, or more exactly super-eminently experiencing [*sur-vivre*] it, of finding for it a universal expression. But of what nature is this universality? It is obvious that it is not the universality of the concept and we are obliged to return to this category of the lived through or experienced [*vécue*] for which—always out of fear of psychologism—M. De Schloezer shows such an incorrigible aversion. "The heart," he writes, "is struck only when the work has been apprehended in its unity by the intelligence. All the rest is physiology. Applied to the aural art, the well known expression must be reversed: nothing exists in sensibility which has not previously existed in the intelligence." As for me, I categorically reject this statement. In the first place because it re-institutes an op-position which is manifestly transcended in the musical experience, as, moreover, in any aesthetic experience of whatever kind. The author clearly postulates that the musician has not necessarily *experienced* the feeling that his work is supposed to translate. But this negative remark is, to my mind, completely fallacious. It is certain that he may not have felt it immediately, but then one must admit that the feeling, instead of "parking" in the zone of experience properly so called, has in some sense transported itself onto the plane of creation that is itself a plane of life, but a superior kind of life, one that is settled [*décante*] and reduced as it were to its *essence*. This word 'essence' takes on a central value here. For my part, I think that the great musician is the one who uncovers essences. And no doubt an essence appears at the same time as a structure but cannot be *reduced* to this structural aspect. One can even say that this essence is not even essence except insofar as it is capable of being experienced; that it appeals in some sort to what we must perhaps call the sympathetic imagination of the listener to experience it for its own sake. I have had the occasion to write elsewhere that there is no creation that is not at the same time an instigation to create, and in fact, the true listener recreates the music that he listens to. But this does not at all mean that he accomplishes for his own sake a certain collection of linked intellectual operations, for example, after the fashion of an apprentice mathematician who re-works a demonstration. Or, more exactly, this interpretation not only does not exhaust the act of appreciative apprehension, it also conceals its specific value. M. De Schloezer goes so far as to say that the "magic" must be eliminated from the perfect musical work, that the music is magic precisely to the extent that it is not music. I could not possibly protest more strongly against this interpretation. I will say exactly the opposite. Music, precisely at the point where it empties out the magical element (whose nature, moreover, we would need to specify), betrays itself, precisely because it gives way to a vain attempt to disincarnate itself. What M. B. de Schloezer calls magic I will call the very flesh of music. And it is through this flesh that music addresses itself to me, who am also a creature of flesh. There is no domain in which Cartesianism is more likely to lead us astray, in which we must more obstinately resist the temptation to form an intellectual, exclusively intellectual notion of purity. But a very pure being is not a disincarnate being, and a musical idea is, precisely, a being.

What vitiates M. de Schloezer's thought from the very beginning, I think, is that for him "to experience music" is to abandon oneself to it voluptuously. But this is only *one way* of experiencing it, the most mediocre, the easiest also, without any doubt. The truth is that this life of music in us has as many nuanced and hierarchized modalities as the life of a feeling, for example, the feeling of love. Otherwise it would be absolutely impossible to understanding what is nevertheless obvious, namely, that there is a musical universe that is as ample as the world of the soul, as unfathomable as metaphysical.

I do not conceal from myself in any way the difficulties raised by an interpretation of this sort. How, you will ask me, can you hope to establish a correspondence between the hierarchy of feelings considered from the point of view of their qualities and the hierarchy of the levels and registers of inspiration? Here lies an immense problem. I can only touch on a solution I would be inclined to give it presently. One would have to begin to disengage the idea of a spiritual hierarchy from all the ethico-social encrustation that covers over common awareness. The authentically spiritual can have only distant connections with a certain conventional good given the stamp of approval either by the academies or by moral manuals. And it is the authentically spiritual alone that is important for us here. But as for me, I do not hesitate, even at the risk of scandalizing certain aesthetes, to think that it is this authentically spiritual that incarnates itself in the highest musical expressions it is given us to apprehend: in Bach, in the Beethoven of the last quartets, in Mozart at his highest and freest. Much more, these great geniuses and a few others—a Schubert, a Brahms, a Fauré—furnish us in flashes with the flaming records of this concrete spirituality that, moreover, we are able to recognize at the level of daily experience, in an inflection, in a look charged with some indefinable, immemorial treasure.

Note

[1] This article originally appeared in *La vie intellectuelle*, vol. IX (April, 1927).

Music and the Reign of the Spirit

It is currently accepted and quite willingly proclaimed that music is the most spiritual of the arts. But what people mean by that, I fear, is only that it is the least material or, more precisely, that the elements with which the musician works, because they are not solid or compact givens, but, on the contrary, sounds, seem less material than those that are formed by the painter or the architect.

It is difficult not to wonder if this "idea", this "cliché" does not rest on a rather deplorable failure to make the proper distinctions. It is quite certain that the philistine tends to imagine the "material" as being something solid or, if you like, something tangible; and it is certainly not an accident that the same word means breath and spirit. But it is no less manifest that a physicist will never admit that matter is less matter in a gaseous than in a solid state. And it is very difficult for the philosopher not to agree with the scientist—although we would have to do violence to ourselves not to recognize in "waves" a certain immateriality. Will someone object that sound cannot be identified with the vibrations to which people want to reduce it and that it exists only for and through consciousness? But are things really any different for color or for form? The more one reflects on the respective domains in which the various arts are practiced, the more it seems absurd to distinguish or hierarchize them [as Hegel does] according to the degree of materiality that is realized in each one.

But that is not all. One would have to attack directly the Cartesian notion according to which the spiritual is defined in opposition to the material (to extension) and after a fashion excludes it from itself. If one rejects this postulate, one will be led to contest that the greater or lesser great value of a particular art is a function of its degree of independence with regard to matter. There is every reason to think that this value can be apprehended in function of an indivisible reality and that Cartesianism tends to make this reality literally inconceivable: I mean, incarnation. There exists no art that is not a modality and, as it were, a potency of incarnation, a potency accompanied by a specific sign character [*indice*].

If there exists a text capable of clarifying the subject that concerns us, it appears in the extraordinary letter that Reiner Maria Rilke wrote on Nov. 13, 1925, to Witold von Hulewicz. "To transmute? Yes.... Such is our mission: to impress this temporary and lifeless earth in us so painfully, so passionately that its essence comes to life again in us, invisible. We are the bees of the invisible. We store up the honey of the visible with abandon to accumulate it in the great golden beehive of the Invisible." Of course, the author of the *Duino Elegies* is here speaking about the poet. But I think that the great idea that is expressed here gives a marvelous account of the decantation which is at the origin of music, of any music worthy of this name. Moreover, it is a matter here of an intelligible operation presenting this singular character of disengaging essences that, after a fashion, can be doubtless reduced to ideal relationships, but which, however, are still freighted with a sensory cargo or another type of speech that adheres indefectibly to what I am inclined to call the very substance of our world and our destiny. And it is precisely through this adherence, that can only be observed but not analyzed, that music, like painting or poetry, is, as it were, an expression radiating from the mystery of incarnation. Without my insisting on it, one sees here, on the one hand, why a mathematical philosophy of music must always be considered as possible and as capable of satisfying an irrefrangible wish of reason. And, on the other hand, why, considered from a point of view more internal and concrete, this same mathematics appears necessarily as insufficient and as foreign to the final secret that music delivers to us in the closest and most chaste of embraces.

* * *

What I would like to attempt to examine in these few pages is the type of adequation that the mind tends to accomplish between itself—between its most intimate requirements—and the original world in which the composer of genius realizes himself and to which he delivers himself over.

The universal is, as it were, the element in which the mind finds its substance and takes flight. Hence I will be justified in wondering what sort of universality music can claim.

It appears to simple reflection that an authentic musical work finds a hearing far beyond the relatively limited zone in which a poem can be fully understood and appreciated (one can in fact ignore the quite deceptive extension that translations into foreign languages make possible). In a general way we must recognize, it seems to me, that poetry remains prisoner of determinations conferred on it by a particular genius of language that is very imperfectly communicable. It is thus practically impossible for someone who is not Russian to appreciate the marvelous quality of the poems of Pushkin, whereas the music of Mussorgsky, for example, does not encounter any barrier of incomprehension in France. I would go even farther and say, while recalling my own experience, that the intimate understanding of *Boris* [*Goudanov*] or *Sunless* makes possible through the more or less opaque veil of the translation a much more intimate and more immediate understanding of certain Russian writers, as though music were capable of filling a veritable function of an interpreter between peoples. There is here, I think, not a mere appearance but a profound reality.

Not without reason one will observe that the plastic arts likewise have no knowledge of this terrible linguistic gulf—and that on this point music thus does not enjoy any real privilege. But what must draw our attention here is the fact that in addition music does indeed seem to be addressed to "the inner man" whom the poet also means to touch.

And we spontaneously have the impression, perhaps essentially quite misleading, that the painter or the sculptor do not address this inner man unless they conclude an onerous and perhaps illicit pact with literature. I will not insist on this point, though there would be matter for extended reflection here. It is quite clear in fact that there exist some painters who are more musical than others, and this hierarchy could be observed even in the greatest. I am not simply alluding to what is meant by the expression "to make colors sing", but to a much more intimate order of relations, consequently much more directly expressible. No one will contradict me if I say, for example, that Watteau is infinitely more a musician than Boucher or Rembrandt than Franz Hals. What makes a difference here is an intimacy that has nothing to do with the sort of intentions only too prevalent in painters of lesser caliber. What is much more obvious is that music does not presuppose, as does painting or sculpture, a preexisting object that the artist gives to himself if he does not encounter it ready made on his path. I am not unaware that the plastic arts tend to free themselves from any model. But one can wonder if this liberation is anything other than an adventure, I would almost say an escapade without a future, and if the reasons that govern it are not most often "intellectual". (I am thinking at this moment of an artist who declared to me that since photography had the task of exactly reproducing all the real, painting was obliged to abandon this reproduction totally. One has difficulty believing that any great painter of the past or even of our time could have let himself be moved by this argument which is clearly based upon a failure to distinguish.)

Even though architecture in a general way creates an entirely new object that exists by itself, it nevertheless presents a certain similarity to music. This is particularly striking if one thinks, for example, of the polyphonic music of Palestrina or of certain fugues of Bach. I think, however, that here too one should not push the comparison too far. Architecture tends by definition to create an object that exists by itself and, as it were, independently of individuals. It does not matter that they stop observing it—and this is so precisely by reason of the properly social function of an edifice of whatever kind. It is thus to the degree that it is in some fashion the most human of the arts that it can attain and even aim at this existence by itself. Here it seems to me there is an antinomy that is fairly rarely remarked upon. But in music one notes that one *can* observe nothing similar, even admitting that it be possible to recommend to the composer—as it was fashionable to say after the war[2]—that he banish all emotion, all subjectivity from his creation. This aberrant conception that has not given birth to any work worthy of memory—and for good reason—can today be filed away without hesitation among the extravagances caused by a sterility that, far from humbly recognizing itself for what it is, intends not only to confer on itself a transcendent justification, but also really and truly to ostracize everything that could even distantly resemble the affirmations of feeling. But once again, even if one agreed that the expression "objective music" means something, one should nonetheless maintain, between the subject and this mode of art at the extreme limit of depersonalization, a much closer mode of dependence than that involved in architectural creation.

The central point on which one must concentrate one's attention is that the architect, like the sculptor, fulfills himself in an object that is realized once and for all and in some fashion introduces itself into the totality of things. The untranslatable German word *Daseyende* expresses perfectly this insertion into an existing web.[3] The musical work of whatever sort has as its essence, it seems, always needing to be performed, that is to say, to be "begun again" [*recommencer*]. Doubtless, this is not absolutely true; nevertheless it is an essential aspect of the truth. The pianist who must interpret opus 111 is each time faced with a new task. His role does not consist in any way of unveiling an object already there—after the fashion of the sacristan in an Italian church pushing aside the curtain hiding from the eyes of the profane (that is to say, non-paying visitors) the altarpiece by Titian or Bellini. Strange as this comparison or this "contrast" [*opposition*] may at first seem, I think it deserves some attention. The material act performed by the sacristan remains entirely exterior to the work that is revealed, whereas, in contrast, opus 111 in its entirety depends and "does not depend" on the performance of the pianist. The pianist cannot be unaware that the work by Beethoven simultaneously possesses an absolute, transcendent existence—and has need of him, hands itself over to him without defense: he can "massacre" it. I think that the performer who is not thus torn in two by these two apparently incompatible assertions proves by this very fact that he is no longer a true artist, but rather a mechanism and tends to become a living gramophone. Moreover, upon reflection it would seem that here there is another antinomy. With a work that by definition remains identically the same and even does not possess in itself any possibility of change, how could one not be led to an interpretation that is itself always identical, that is to say, stereotyped? It seems on reflection that the more superficial a work is, the more this question turns out to be in fact soluble.[4] A superficial work, doubtless, rightfully allows a type of perfect and invariable interpretation. In contrast, the deeper a work is, the more an inexhaustible sum of intimate experience is integrated into it, the more one can conceive that it provides in any particular performance that takes place in time only a certain partial aspect of itself, such that the multiplicity of successive performances, each one considered as a qualitatively specified event, would find its foundation, its justification, its guarantee in the very essence of the work of genius. I limit myself to this assuredly too brief sketch of a solution because it allows us to see how, in the musical reality, an antinomy from which logically it seems impossible to escape, can find itself transcended (rather than resolved).

These remarks prepare us to recognize the analogy, too rarely noticed, I think, between music and virtue. Of course here I adopt the point of view of the interpreter. One would subsequently need to attempt to consider the work from the perspective of the composer; but here the obscurity becomes almost impenetrable. The essence of a work is not exhausted in a performance any more than the essence of a virtue of whatever kind can be enclosed within the limits of a particular act. The virtue is beyond the act as the work is beyond the performance, beyond each performance, and yet in a sense the virtue is immanent in the act as the work is immanent in the operation by which the performer reveals it. We must beware of the pianist who assures us that he "possesses" opus 111, just as we mistrust the Pharisee who declares his generosity the way one declares a possession, a revenue. In both cases we are by definition beyond any possible possession, in a domain where the risk always remains absolute precisely because the gift is total.

Only in both cases, let us observe it carefully, there exists a hither side where it becomes once again possible to say correctly: "I possess." This is the domain of virtuosity in all its forms. And in making this observation, I become aware not without amusement of the very instructive relationship between the two words, 'virtue' and 'virtuosity'. Here, as always, speech is marvelously significant and sagacious.

But of course the situation of the composer is quite different. It is even, literally, "incomparable". For the composer—and for him alone—something has been realized or obtained that truly presents the seal of the definitive. It scarcely matters here that the conditions in which this discovery takes place are infinitely variable. I use this word 'discovery' designedly, for it is very clear to my eyes that the musician "finds" much rather than "invents". But we do not need to wonder if the idea—the melody—springs forth completely formed, completely constituted or if the artist frees it, extracts it laboriously from a matrix that presents itself first as an aural nebula. The only important thing is the act of recognition by which the musician assures himself that the idea, "this idea," entirely determinate, is indeed the one he was seeking, that he was waiting for, that he intuited. One cannot say, moreover, that he possesses it straight away. It astonishes him, it dazzles him, like a star suddenly discovered in the depths of the sky. It overwhelms him, I would even say; and it does this to the extent that he can in no way be aware that he produced it. It is him—and it is not him. (It would be better to speak of the "maternity" of the artist than of his paternity. It is only a pseudo-sociological prejudice linked to an absurd human respect that prevents us from doing so.) The idea presents itself thus as an answer or as an affirmation. But what deserves all our attention is the fact that this affirmation will be transformed for the performer and for the listener into a powerful call, into a pressing invitation to re-create and to assume. Here, moreover, we are in a domain that is in some degree common to music and poetry. If I admire a poem, I feel the need to make it my own, to incorporate it, as it were, into my own substance by memorizing. It is as if, thanks to this effort, I manage to reduce the painful exteriority that, in spite of everything, detracts from *possession* as such. But one will grant, I think, that in the case of music participation is much more active and more felt than it is with the reciter in the case of poetry. It is not only that the material effort is greater, that much more significant patience and perseverance are required. There is a difference of quality, it seem to me, between the two modes of assimilation. At the risk of scandalizing some poet, I would be inclined to say that the elements of which the poem is made are often more "given", much more capable of interior renewal that those that constitute the art-song or the sonata. Could one not observe that here there is a hierarchy in the gift of self, in the sacrifice? A Horowitz, a Gieseking, a Menuhin or a Heifetz—to take examples from among the living[5]—give themselves, in spite of everything, in quite a different way than can be the case with a tragic actor reciting a poem, however beautiful.

Here an objection could be made. Does not the tragedian in the very exercise of his art, the tragedian playing and no longer reciting, also sacrifice himself to the character he is playing? Is the sacrifice here not absolute? No doubt. But I think that here we are led to make an important remark that permits us to penetrate very far into the territory that we are trying to explore. What happens in the theatre is a veritable substitution: in some sort (perhaps not absolutely) the personality of Sarah Bernhart or of Eleanora Duse must disappear before that of Phaedra or Nora—not absolutely, because into the performance there must pass, in spite of everything, a certain irreducible quality that belongs to the temperament of either of these great artists. This quality, however, makes the transition only as a deception, as contraband—because in reality there is, doubtless, nothing in common between what Sarah Bernhart could be and the idea that we must form, for example of Racine's heroine. And one must add that this infiltration can occur only insofar as the character is not perfectly determinate and presents, as it were, lacunae. In music there is nothing similar. I am speaking at this moment, of course, of "pure music." Lyric music poses special problems, of an extreme complexity and in certain respects "impure" (in that they can only be resolved by compromises that are most often precarious). At the root of dramatic art there is a fiction, a "let's pretend" which could never in any way find a place in musical art (or in architecture). And therein lies, I think, its essential and marvelous superiority. It is by this path and this path alone that it is perhaps possible to enter into this reality, mysterious above all others, and all the more mysterious in that it is the more incontestable: musical reality.

Here, of course, we cannot fail to come up against a difficulty that I will not attempt to minimize. To interpret Chopin, you will say, is to interpret his feelings and in some manner to mime them. It is thus to act "as if" one were Chopin, that is to pretend, like the actor who plays Arnolphe or Nero. But this objection allows us precisely to recognize and to indicate the essential universality that distinguishes the musical genius. Chopin is Chopin, and a great musician of whatever sort is himself only to the degree to which it is not "his" feelings, in the, so to say, exclusionary [*privatif*] meaning of this word, that his art expresses. He is himself only to the degree to which he establishes himself through musical expression far beyond, infinitely beyond his own feelings, in a zone where he joins an infinity of souls and becomes their spokesperson. Only, here too, let us be very careful. There is no question of allowing that this expression merely translates after the fact states of soul that pre-existed it. Here is the profound difference between the musician and the writer. These states of soul take form only through the expression that the composer seems to put at their service. Although, *a posteriori*, the listener can scarcely fail to imagine through an actual temporal illusion that he felt them first. The truth is that a Chopin, a Wagner, a Debussy are conquerors of an inner world and that one entirely misunderstands their role, their originality in considering them in any other way. But nothing is more difficult than to manage to grasp exactly what the annexations are that we owe to them and to understand their import.

Precisely to the extent that we use a spatial terminology, we make ourselves incapable of "recalling" what is in question. For reasons that the philosophy of Bergson manages perfectly to illumine, we are always likely to imagine an enrichment, an extensive accretion. This mode of imagining is already revealed to be quite inadequate when one considers the development of a particular science that could rather be compared to the development of a living organism, with all that it implies of differentiation, of functional specialization. For an art like music it is not even in the biological order that one can hope to find, I will not say equivalencies, but distant approximations.

But what appears to me remarkable in the continuation of the preceding observations is that the more one attempts to think here in terms of generalities, the more one loses contact with the mystery one proposes to grasp. It is as though this mystery were suddenly reduced to an evanescent mirage. Yes, this mystery loses its density, that is to say, its reality, only to recover, in contrast, its true dimensions as soon as attention is concentrated on any particular work, any particular melody where the "current" of an authentic inspiration flows. To be sure, to speak here of current is still to use a metaphor that may appear arbitrary. And yet thumb through, for example, the complete edition of Schubert's songs. I challenge you not to feel literally the impression that in a great number of these *Lieder*, "nothing happens". And then suddenly a hitherto unheard of tone makes itself heard. In what does this difference consist? I am inclined to say that it is the contrast between the inhabited and the uninhabited. But inhabited by whom and by what? Just as a moment ago we had to be wary of the pitfalls of space, here we must protect ourselves from the temptations of grammar, of a grammatical substantialism. In the objective world we are obliged to distinguish between the being that is present and the presence itself, the fact of presence. But it is precisely this distinction that becomes impracticable here, or, more exactly, that loses all character other than verbal.

Here we are getting on to an idea that seems to me central to such a degree that I despair of formulating it rigorously. In formulating it one is in danger in fact of degrading it. Ths idea is that the musical mystery is the very mystery of presence. And here we must refer to what is most intimate in the commerce between beings. In the spiritual meaning of the word, 'presence' cannot be reduced to the fact of being there. Presence is not given; I would say rather that it is revealed. And it is once again Bergson's philosophy that comes to our aid here. A being is present to us when it opens itself up to us. And this in no way implies that it is placed in next to us in space, just as, inversely, it can happen that our neighbor, even if we see him, if we touch him, remains entirely closed for us—in spite of the normal communications, the social exchanges that are established between us. Everyday reality, precisely to the extent that it is usual, that it offers for our action and commentaries handles that are assured, locatable, countable, is for us as if it were not; and we ourselves, moreover, in so far as we are in contact with it, are strangers to ourselves. Common life is thus reduced to a dialogue between absences that condition each other. In the same way, when my eyes glance over this or that art-song of Schubert that posterity has been right to have ignored, when I listen to it interiorly, I move within a neutral element that, because it provides me no resistance, could not possibly reserve for me any revelation. I am in an *apeiron*, not an infinite but an indefinite that lends itself to a thousand *unbestimmte* [German, 'indeterminate'] combinations, but all in theory foreseeable, and all destined to undo themselves even as they form themselves. This *apeiron* is only the transposition onto the aesthetic plane of everyday banality whence it seems that nothing can emerge. Boredom, if one looks carefully at it, is a reaction against this banality, against this *apeiron*, but a reaction that is impotent to transform itself into structure and consequently to surpass a stage of pure negativity. But what I call presence is the sudden emergence, unforeseeable, salvific, of a form that is not simply traced, but wedded, that is to say, re-created from within and in which an entire experience, instead of being lost, instead of being scattered like sand and dust, concentrates itself, affirms itself, proclaims itself.

But perhaps there is not essentially any appreciable difference between presence and freedom. I have written somewhere that the free act is the liberating act. Now, it is precisely in presence that the spirit frees itself from the *apeiron* that is pure dissemination and mournful repetition. And here I will make so bold as to call upon an experience that, however humble, nonetheless presents to my eyes an inestimable and even crucial value: the experience of musical improvisation.

How many times, at moments when I felt myself cut off from myself, that is, from my profound roots, and as it were absorbed by the everyday, as soon as I sat down at the piano and let my hands wander over the keys, have I not had, as it were, the physical feeling of sails catching the wind, of a heart that begins to beat once again. This phenomenon of taking hold of oneself again [*ressaisissement*] is one of the most mysterious that I know, and it is, in a certain sense, mystery itself. I can affirm without hesitation that it was almost always during these periods that, in my ordinary sphere of activity, I felt the most blocked, the most exhausted, that it was given me to feel in the most intense, immediate way, the extraordinary power of recuperation that is attached to music, as if it were restoring me to myself in an independent world, a world without discernible communication with a sort of spiritual "no man's land," a sordid and desolate suburb in which my soul a few instants earlier had been dragging itself along. What could the intrinsic value of these improvisations have been, improvisations that have never been written down? I have no idea, and I will never know. It is a question that, to tell the truth, I am even obliged not to ask myself. The improvisations were destined only for myself and took on their meaning only in relation to a certain restoration of my inner being that, it seems to me, could not have taken place without them. No doubt they are of an essence very analogous, very comparable to prayer. And here there is a point that just in itself would be worth a long study. Likewise, there is no doubt in my eyes that a great and exalted music is "for men in general" what this salvific improvisation was able to be for the helpless individual that I was. No doubt the spiritual function of music consists essentially in restoring man to himself. But to inquire into this *sibimet ipsi* [Latin reduplicative, 'to oneself oneself' and thus 'to one's very self'"] and, as it were, to expand its meaning is the job of metaphysics, of theology. To restore man to himself is in truth to restore him to God. When he was the director of the Beaux-Arts my father, having to give a speech for the inauguration of the monument for César Franck in front of Sainte-Clotilde, spoke of the great musicians as our "guarantors" ["*répondants*"]. There is here, I am firmly convinced, a profound truth and one that his passionate love for music allowed him to sense, although Christian faith had not been allotted to him, or at least he believed himself detached from it. All authentic musical creation is a mediation that takes place in the bosom of a being so incomprehensibly divided and, as it were, split, that is, man engaged in time. Never will one be able to meditate too deeply on the marvelous affinity that connects music and memory. There is a hierarchy of types of music just as there are levels to memory, from the most mechanical to the most intimate, from the one that is a mere "reproduction" to the one that is a "re-living" ["*revivre*"] and a "super-living" ["*survivre*"]. And it is in virtue of these affinities that the most sublime creations of the musician, of Bach, Mozart or Beethoven, present themselves to the mind as a pledge of eternity, like the active inmost depths of our life of thought.

Notes

[1] This article appeared originally in *Revue Internationale de Musique*, 1940.

[2] 1914-18.

[3] *Translator's note*: Hegel used the term *Daseyn*, literally 'being there', to signify 'something' in contrast to 'others'. Heidegger used it to signify human reality as the place (*Da*) where Being (*Seyn* or *Sein*) appears in the midst of beings as revealed through the web of an inter-human world.

[4] *Translator's note*: Marcel's text has ***insoluble***, but, unless we misunderstand what is involved here, that has to be a typo.

[5] The article appeared in 1940.

Music According to
Saint Augustine[1]

As everyone knows, **Saint Augustine** left us the first six books of a treatise on music that his entrance into holy orders prevented him from finishing. Mr. Davenson, the author of an important work on the bishop of Hippo and the end of ancient culture, attempts, in this remarkably dense little book published by the Cahiers du Rhone, to consider anew the musical theology of St. Augustine in its entirety. "I am concerned here with thought, not with history. I want to help my reader discover what music is in truth, not to reconstruct what St. Augustine thought about it between 387 and 391."

Adopting as his own the traditional definition of music as the art of good modulation, St. Augustine observes that the movement that constitutes music is related to the movement of the dancer who moves solely for the beauty of his gesture, whereas the movement of the craftsman, of the potter, for example, will be judged by the object worked on that will be produced by his hands. It follows, M. Davenson notes, that music, aural movement, ceases to be music precisely at the moment when we cease to locate its profound value and its proper perfection in this interior and immanent meaning that the musician's soul perceives naturally.

But if things are thus, how could the composer Arthur Lourie, to whom the author dedicates this treatise, declare one day in his presence: "Art is an imitation; music also is an imitation"?

The contradiction vanishes only if one admits, along with Platonism, that the model in question here does not belong to the domain of sensory experience. In this understanding, musical beauty is thus only an echo of spiritual beauty. Has St. Augustine not strongly emphasized that, although sound properly so called is developed within time, musical beauty remains immobile, *sine tempore stans in quodam secreto et alto silentio* ["without time, standing in some secret and exalted silence"]? The being of the melody is grasped only in the synthesis represented by the particular memory [*souvenir*] of the whole, in which the faculty of memory [*mémoire*] takes in the echo of each one of the successive sounds modified, illumined by the neighborhood of each of the others. It is only in the memory that the melody exists truly with a purely spiritual existence, freed from the inexorable flowing away of duration. When I play, it is clear that I am trying to reproduce, always approximately to be sure, the silent music that lives in my memory. The paradox of sight-reading, I will add, consists in the quasi-simultaneity of the act by which this silent music constitutes itself in the soul itself and the act by which it incarnates itself and takes on material form in sound. Let us say further that auditory experience, in causing this music to pass through time, allows me to embrace it, to savor it, to enjoy it. And once the playing is over, the music remains more living than it was before. It has taken on body. To the latent memory that I possessed of it, another memory has substituted itself, one much more present, more vivid, still vibrating from the recent hearing. It is while thinking of this living unity, this global perception that persists in me when the strings have grown quiet, that St. Augustine speaks of a music of judgment that alone is true music, because it alone brings this emotion and this happiness that give music its value and its worth for us. All musical experience reflects, moreover, the tragic tension implicit in the struggle against time, the contrast between the musical matter that, through the actualized sound, exists only in the present, and its form that can constitute its unity only beyond duration within the immobile and silent judgment. Practice is here like a stammering attempt to triumph over this antinomy and to create in consciousness a deceitful state that is like an *ersatz* of eternity.

We must go even further and observe that it is no doubt impossible to feel inhabited and animated by a new piece of music without having the feeling of recognizing it, without discovering that one was waiting for it and that it was preformed, as it were, in this very awaiting. This is what gives to certain encounters their "unforgettable and almost charismatic character." Let us not speak here of reminiscence. Let us say only that "the musician's soul that participates, according to its capacity, in the limitless fecundity of the spirit develops spontaneously in itself an inner music, one of a subtle essence, anterior to meaning—a music that the work of the composer and later the play of the instruments will imitate as well as they can, but always imperfectly, even though this incomplete participation suffices to ennoble the result of their efforts and to establish its beauty." In the composer himself one will thus find at the very beginning "the intuition of a musical piece not yet incarnate.... It is by contemplating it that the musician will see it appear successively before being able to get hold, through the notation, of each of the fragments of the future work.... He imitates with audible forms the silent music that he discovers in the abstract distance [*l'abstrait*] of his heart."

Before going further I would like to propose here a few remarks. How could one not wonder if an interpretation like this does not excessively intellectualize the mysterious process we are trying to describe? Mr. Davenson himself admits that the expression "music of judgment" is inadequate. But, he says, how would language, that very fragile tool, not break when it comes into contact with this crystal-hard and sparkling reality? But I fear that he himself makes himself guilty of a more serious imprecision when he says that the musician contemplates his inner music. What strikes me, I admit, is the insufficiency of the phenomenological analysis of this attempt to reconstitute musical becoming. I cannot help fearing that it can be explained by the fact that Mr. Davenson, philosopher or theologian, remains the prisoner of certain Platonic or Scholastic categories. The very expression "musical theology" cannot fail to awaken some quite lively misgivings in this regard.

To begin with, I believe that without hesitation one must reject Lourie's formulation. Music, whatever it may be, is *not* an imitation. We have nothing to gain, but on the contrary everything to lose by interpreting as a relationship of model to copy the connection that tends to establish itself between what I will call, for lack of a better term, "musical being" and its incarnation. One could not possibly, I think, protest strongly enough against the interpretation according to which the birth of the idea and of its melody could be assimilated to the grasping of an object, however interior one may imagine it. Only what one must recognize is that reflection, in attempting to picture for itself retrospectively what is felt as gestation and as birth, ends up almost inevitably transposing into the *figurative register* what has, however, no reality other than on the level of the *experienced* [*vécue*].

The musical being is a *presence* and the first concern of the phenomenologist will have to be to emphasize the impossibility in which we find ourselves of dissociating in fact the present content on the one hand, and the mode of presence, the way of being present on the other. Here I am for my part convinced that it is from the order of relations of being to being that all references must be drawn. The presence of the Other can be discrete or, on the contrary, despotic; it can be insinuating or invasive; it can be obscuring or illuminating. In any case, it is felt much more than it is contemplated. I will go further: it is probable that if it were contemplated, it would no longer be a presence at all. For that matter, I am the first to deplore the inadequacy of the word 'to feel' [*ressentir*]. It is manifestly the wrong word to express the innumerable real relations that an individual being is capable of developing in relationship to this other individual existence that is called melody, relations all having to do with a *pure erotic* that remains to be created.

Even at that, we would have reservations about the use of the word 'relation'. The term 'participation' seems to me infinitely preferable. There is in fact a relation between isolated elements within a certain visual field, or within a field of thought that is, after all, only transposition and continuation. Now precisely here we are in an area that can in no way be assimilated to a comparable field. One could say that the common contrast between to be or to exist on the one hand, and to represent on the other, is radically abolished. Let us say further that the musician's soul is a haunted soul. But it is impossible to bring in experiences like those of haunting or simply of encounter without breaking the intellectual categories of which, on the contrary, one remains a prisoner when one speaks either of music of judgment or quite simply music of intuition. The simple fact that this last expression is filled with Orphic references should suffice to make it suspect for us.

However, Mr. Davenson is perfectly right to warn us about two contrary dangers. "One must," he says, "neither lose music by holding oneself beneath it, as do the carnal men who confuse music with the low emotions that it excites in them, nor go beyond it by transcending it…. To the first group one must show that music can be of a mental order without ceasing for all that to be real. But one must not either, like the second group, pass beyond the limit and situate music outside of sound." It is assuredly very true that music must tend to incorporate itself into our spiritual substance in such a way that we no longer need to hear it performed. But it nonetheless remains contributor to an inner hearing that seems indeed still to require a certain intervention of the body. But by what kind of aberration does Mr. Davenson take Dukas' *Ariane et Barbe-Bleue* as an example of carnal music? *Ariane et Barbe-Bleue*, that is to say, the work that pushes as far as can be the process of sublimation by which the auditory jewel is spiritualized to the point of becoming the pure melody of the soul that transcends itself, that enters into itself, rising above everything, even the impulse of pity which inclines it to come to the aid of the enslaved creature. One should not say to oneself that this and only this is merely the subject of the work. It is its very essence. The final scene, which is one of the summits of music, has constituted for an entire generation—my own, the generation of Henri Franck, of Andre George, and of so many others—one of the most undeniable witnesses of a musical reality that Mr. Davenson is perhaps too inclined to recognize in its fullness only where the Christian affirmation is at least implicit.

In truth, it is always infinitely perilous to speak about what one has not expounded and taken up. One is invariably in danger of pronouncing excommunications that fall back only on one's self. Hence I will not receive without the most serious reservations the condescending appraisals that Mr. Davenson gives in passing to Wagner's master works. That the continuous melody bores him is a fact, a simple idiosyncrasy. But by what right does one think he can devalue a musical experience as outstanding as the one of which Bayreuth has been the home and still will remain so for a long time? I willingly admit that Wagner does not allow himself to be easily integrated into a musical theology like the one Mr. Davenson has sketched out. But does this not simply prove that this theology is infinitely too narrow and too simple, and that it is not simply premature but abusive to want to encapsulate the world of musical experiences within safe dogmatic formulas? Above I used the term 'phenomenology'. In my opinion it is there and there only that it is possible today to find solid ground for a philosophy of musical experience.

To be sure, Mr. Davenson is right a thousand times over to say that music is neither the foolish game of a dilettante "who diverts himself by following with a jaded eye the flickering reflections of the ephemeral nor the illusion of a misguided soul that nourishes itself with an appearance and with a simulacrum of an absolute." But it seems to me dangerous to add that "it is or rather must be one of the means that a soul already sufficiently reformed [*redressée*] can, if it is wise—and, if such is its vocation, *must*—use to purify itself and to reform itself further in its re-ascent and return towards God." Now this is a dogmatic affirmation that may well satisfy the Catholic as Catholic or even the Christian as Christian but which, from the strictly musical point of view, is likely to seem not only gratuitous but absolutely improper. It seems to me that a work such as [Debussy's] *Pelléas et Mélisande*, which I admire as much as Mr. Davenson, cannot be regarded without being arbitrary as a stage in an ascesis or a stage in a purifying dialectic tending towards the Ineffable. Like any authentic masterpiece, it presents a certain *autarkia*. It is from a point of view that is absolutely foreign to itself, in the strong sense of the term, foreign to its essence, that we can possibly be led to recognize that it is capable of helping a soul to find herself and to encounter the One outside of Whom no ultimate accomplishment is possible.

I will say then that one is adopting a perspective that is complete foreign to that of the artist as such, whether he is called Mozart or Beethoven, Chopin, Fauré or Wagner, in treating music as a means to a spiritual end, even if it were the highest of all. The ethicist and the theologian are in danger of treading here on territory that could not possibly belong to them, and it is always to be feared that this intrusion may bring with it as a consequence the excommunication of some genius of the first magnitude, denounced as a heretic. To be sure, one can only admire the sublime text of St. Maximus the Confessor, to which Mr. Davenson refers us. But the "silence of the spirit," if it surpasses all music, does not seem to be—and for this very reason—to be able to be conceived as the absolute touchstone of musical creation. *Sile coram Domino et expecta eum*, ["Be silent before the Lord and await him"] we read in the Psalms. But this exhortation could not possibly provide us with the principle of a "musical morality." Music in the final analysis can find its form and its supreme authority only in itself.

* * *

(Following upon this article, an exchange of letters took place between H. Davenson and Gabriel Marcel that appeared in the June issue of *Confluences*. We reproduce Marcel's letter.)

May 10, 1943. Dear Sir: Mr. Tavernier has passed on to me your very interesting letter. It moves me; it disturbs me; it forces me to question myself. Where exactly is our disagreement located? Or rather, what in me felt the need to protest, with a perhaps excessive vehemence, certain of the positions you took in your book? In reading you, I had the impression that you were causing harm to the autonomy of the musician or of musical experience. And on this point I cannot say that you reassure me. In your letter you introduce the moralist. To what degree is it legitimate to judge a musical work as *a moralist*? I think the whole problem is there. We must leave to the side the distinction between the apophatic and the cataphatic. I once wrote, "When one speaks of God it is not of God that one is speaking." It is thus difficult to criticize me for being ignorant of the legitimacy and the value of apophatic theology.... To judge as a moralist.... Let us take an example. I don't think that anyone can admire more than I do the genius of Mussorgsky, but I distrust those who praise the spirit of poverty in his music. It is in the name of the spirit of poverty that Maritain once emphasized, in my opinion in an extravagant way, the contribution of poor Satie. And this is where you may end up if you judge as a "moralist." Inversely: you speak of rhetoric with regard to Wagner. I would admit up to a point that there is in Wagner a misuse of development that at times wearies and taxes us. But this abuse is comparable to the luxuriance of certain plants that is also overwhelming. Can nature be likened to a rhetor? I was recently re-reading certain passages of the *Ring Cycle*. I was literally confounded by the immediate power of certain themes to dominate—as immediate, without any doubt, as that of a melody of *Pelléas*. If one judges Wagner as "a moralist," one is in danger of not wishing or not being able to do justice to this aspect of his genius, an aspect, however, that is primordial. That would be as outrageous an abuse as one becomes guilty of when one praises to the skies the *Contrerimes* of Toulet or the *Calligrammes* of Apollinaire while declaring that we need retain of Hugo only a few scattered lines.

I dwell on these examples because they seem crucial to me. To tell the truth, what separates us is not the doctrines that we may profess about Being or even about the human condition. On the contrary, on essential points we are probably very close to being in agreement. No, the divergence is here in our attitudes with regard to the musical phenomenon itself. The expressions I have used are perhaps inadequate. I am as far as possible from adhering to the notion of pure music such as the Stravinsky of 1920-25 conceived it. I would even go so far as to say that music worthy of the name is always laden with truth. Like every expression, music is a restitution, a releasing of what one has breathed in. It can be appreciated only if it is intimately experienced. To appreciate it is first of all to make it your own. But the judgment of the moralist consists much less in assuming than in stamping with approval or refusing. It is pronounced from without. The one who declares it places himself, I fear, in a sphere that is in no wise the one in which music develops itself, the one in which there comes to fruition a strange passion, the mysterious gestation that is the musician's.

In short, what I fear above all is the intrusion (camouflaged) of non-music in the very heart of music. It seems to me inevitable if we grant the moralist the right to speak. To be sure, there is an ethics interior to musical creation, a strictly personal ethics and pretty much intransmissible. And we see at once when the musician has sinned against his own ethics. But this is not the kind of ethics you are concerned about.

This is all that I can say today. It would be interested to know what position this or that musician would adopt with regard to our debate....

Note
[1] This article orginally appeared in *Confluences*, no. 2, 1943.

Response to the Inquiry into "Musical Images"[1]

Boris de Schloezer published ten or so years ago in *La Revue musicale* a few articles entitled, if I remember correctly, "In Search of Musical Reality." I hasten to add that the solution he outlined did not at all satisfy me and has always seemed to me infinitely too intellectual. I think that one understands Bach on the basis of the *Passions* and the *Cantatas*, not on the basis of the *Well Tempered Clavier* and *the Art of the Fugue*. But the question asked in these articles is of a kind that has always interested me. The very term 'musical reality' is one of those expressions I will never give up at any price. The musician has always appeared to me as one who introduces the listener into a certain world which is his own. There is no doubt nothing more foolish and even nothing more impracticable than to attempt to describe the world of a Fauré or of a Debussy, since description can only be exercised on an object existing in space. The world it is a matter of here is essentially a certain way of apprehending the one and only Reality. It is a seizing hold of. Even at that, one must see that this seizing is at once passive and active. It is a way of apprehending the real—yes, no doubt; but it is also, and even more profoundly, a way of being captured, of being embraced or enveloped by this reality that surpasses us on all sides. This seems to me of an extreme importance, and allows me to treat fairly all the idealist attempts to give an account (by whisking it out of sight) of what is the most original and the most essential in musical reality. I do not hesitate to think that this experience has contributed very powerfully to establishing certain of the metaphysical landmarks around which my thought is ordered. I will indicate here only one point, but it is one that seems to me to be essential. Nowhere better than in music can one understand that the universal cannot be reduced to what is valid for a thought in general. What is more, the expression "thought in general" has absolutely no meaning here. Nevertheless, it is only too clear that the musical work, the musical idea is in no way relative to an isolated subject enclosed within its own states of consciousness. On the contrary, there is room here for real encounters. And it is in function of these encounters that the musical reality defines itself, not at all with regard to a disincarnate reason developing according to an inflexible dialectic.

If now I attempt to define more precisely what the specific contribution of French music in our day may have been for me, it seems to me that I would want to center it on the values of intimacy (in contrast, for example, to the cosmic intention that animates the work of Wagner). But these values of intimacy should certainly not be understood in the rather restrictive meaning this word takes on when one thinks of Schumann or of the chamber music Brahms. To take only two examples, illustrious ones however: *Pelleas* and *Penelope* show us, it seems to me, that what I would call the index of intimacy can be attached to great lyrical and dramatic works in which a whole universe of panoramas, of illuminations, of inspirations [*paysages, de lueurs, de souffles*] is evoked. In my opinion, there is a lesson here whose significance is inexhaustible, not only for the musician, but also for the philosopher and the playwright....

Note

[1] This article appeared originally in *Images Musicales*, October, 1945.

Music and the Marvelous[1]

If one sticks with the categories of the historian and considers exclusively the development of so-called sophisticated music in the West, one will be led to hold that the Marvelous made its appearance in the speech of sounds only at a rather recent date, probably with the German Romantics—the Schubert of *Der Erlkönig* and of *Doppelgänger*, the Weber of *Freyschütz* and *Oberon*. One will note on the other hand that in Wagner this language unfolds and at the same time interiorizes itself infinitely, but without preserving anything of the naiveté that is nevertheless essential to it. Was not the Russian contribution to consist to a large extent in reestablishing it at once in its ingenuousness and its primitive opulence? One can see this clearly in the Rimsky-Korsakov of *Schéherazade*, *Sadko* and *Kitège*, and also in the Liadov of *Baba-Yaga*, and in many others. However, the ingenuousness is here intended, deliberate; moreover, it is sufficient to say that it is deceitful, that it is based upon artifice. It is much rather in a Moussorgsky that we discover the sense of the authentically marvelous, in spite of the absence of any fairy apparatus, of any apparatus whatever. It streams down in *The Nursery* as in *Boris* and in the *Khovantchina* and in numerous scattered songs. This is because the Marvelous is the human soul itself, the soul that is a miracle by its very existence, and more intimately still because it leaves a wake of hope in a world of misery and death. The Debussy of *Pelléas* and of the *Nocturnes* circles around this obvious, properly magical truth. But no doubt he is too essentially an artist for the Marvelous to spring forth in him as a source. It is as though he harnesses it and develops its sinuous derivatives. One can say the same of the Ravel of *Ma Mère l'Oye*. Almost everywhere essentially, save in Moussorgsky and the very early Prokofiev, the drama is the same. The sophisticated musician in acclimatizing the Marvelous humanizes it and in some sort denatures it. But we must add that this half-betrayal is perhaps necessary, at least for the "civilized" person, for perhaps it is by this indirect route that those who have forgotten the language of the fairies can rediscover at least some of its inflections. For the civilized person, I say, since the primitive, when he is a musician, communicates directly with the Marvelous through the chance that an age-old tradition has transmitted to him along with life.

One would need, moreover, to dig much more deeply into this matter. And one would then discover that the Marvelous is essentially music itself, for, if it is not charm and magic, music is nothing but mathematics or scholasticism. In music the oppositions are abolished that rule inexorably the universe in which our narrow and precarious action is engaged. It is thus that, thanks to an network of mediations, of an unspeakable tenuousness and perfection, a *fairy space* is constituted within music in which the near and the far pass into each other, in which, through the irresistible efficacy of analogical correspondences, every note, every chord evokes an infinity of others. And the composer appears to himself sometimes as if, after the manner of characters in fairy tales, he were following a mysterious path at the end of which there is waiting for him a treasure or a revelation. In an age like ours when religious faith in its fullness is the possession of only a small number, the increasing dominance of music over so many disaffected hearts can be explained perhaps because music itself, in the precise meaning of the word, becomes religion. That is to say, it rejoins the bonds between the soul and the Marvelous within that is its principle and its depths, bonds that a dazzling [*aveuglantes*] science and technology seem, on the contrary, intent on dissolving.

Note
[1] This article originally appeared in *Plaisir de France*, December, 1948.

Meditation on Music[1]

I do not know if I am mistaken but it seems to me difficult if not impossible to speak *in general* of the relations between music and literature. At most a writer can hope to show—and only approximately—what a musical work that nourished him has been or meant in his life.

In this issue of *La Revue musicale* devoted to fifty years of French music, how could I not choose [Debussy's?] *Pelléas et Mélisande* to attempt to specify the place that such a work has occupied in my life? To *Pelléas* I should, moreover, add [Dukas'] *Ariane et Barbe-Bleue*. For it is a fact that these two works, at a particular period, constituted for me a sort of diptych that was, so to speak, inseparable. I do not think I am exaggerating when I say that no literary work of whatever kind, neither at that time nor even perhaps later, has held the rank of this diptych. Of course it goes without saying for me that here I am speaking exclusively about music. I never participated in the cult of Maeterlinck [the poet whose work furnished the libretto for *Pelléas* and *Ariane*] neither as a moralist nor as a playwright. This does not allow me, however, to consider as negligible the poet's share in these two lyric works since it is he who provided their foundation.

Pelléas imposed itself on me completely only from the moment when, having got a hold of the sheet music for piano and voice, I carefully sight-read it. On first hearing, the work had given me only a rather indistinct general impression. The revelation occurred only at the piano. I say 'revelation'—and it is the only appropriate word—for actually it was in no way a simple emotional disturbance, any more, of course, than it was an intellectual discovery. What seems to me precisely so important in such an experience is that, due to a rudimentary psychology, the contrasts we have created between our faculties reveal themselves here to be absolutely empty of meaning. At the risk of betraying what we have intimately experienced, we are constrained to go beyond such categories. Moreover, this has been

true for me—and I imagine for everybody else—regarding all my
musical discoveries, whether it was a cantata of Bach, a quartet of
Beethoven or an opera of Wagner. But in the case of *Pelléas* and of
Ariane, of which I will speak below, there was this. I found myself in
the presence of a certain perfectly individualized world, into which I
was entering literally on equal footing. To be sure, these expressions
have a metaphorical character, but I do not see any other expression
that can convey this experience. It seems to me for that matter, that,
between the terms 'revelation' and 'world' there exists a veritable correlation. What presents itself to us as a *world* can only *reveal* itself,
and the reverse is no doubt just as true. I will note, moreover, that
things are the same for the sensory world; but that if, at the origin,
this world is *revealed* (and I do not at all give to this world a strictly
religious meaning, or at least a confessional one), due to habitua-
tion and enslavement to practical matters, this revelation gradually
obliterates itself. There is, I think, a profound analogy between the
world the artist reveals to us and the world of primordial experience:
the experience of the child, the experience that it is given to us to
rediscover in lightning flashes and probably in all case with love, and
not necessarily the love of a human being.

I do not know if I am being misled, as one can always fear, by an *a
posteriori* reconstruction, but it does seem to me that nowhere more
than in *Pelléas* have I become aware of this primordial element. This
is surely due in large part to the way in which nature is present in this
work. I am thinking both of the breath of the forest in the Prelude
and of the evocation, so sober and so irresistible, of the Sea, of the
passage, in the scene of the gardens at the end of Act I, or again of
the sea grotto or of the emergence from underground into the light
of noon. As I am writing these lines I observe with amazement that
deep within me all of that is not moved, is not changed, has in no way
undergone the withering action of time. But on the other hand I must
recognize the almost absolute impossibility in which I still find myself
of conferring, if I may say so, a status on these realities that have thus
penetrated into my life, and to define, were it only approximately,
the relationship they have with my being. Nothing, moreover, shows
better, I think, the crude insufficiency of our usual categories. Dare

I say, moreover, that on however philosophical a plane, the essential role played by music in my existence could well have consisted, if one considers it negatively, in derailing a certain speculative conformism. And I will not tire of repeating, beyond the labels that professional classifiers have attached to my thought, that it is this anti-conformism that is the fundamental note in all my work, however paradoxical this may seem to those who wish to situate me *on the Right*.

But on reflection it does seem to me that it is in the perspective of music and of what I will perhaps dare to call musical truth that I can best express the essence of this non-conformism. Of course, it may be tempting at first blush to appeal here to the great memory of Bergson. And, to be sure, I could never state too strongly my gratitude towards this genius that is today sometimes so stupidly, so hatefully misunderstood. But perhaps one must speak rather of analogy than of identity in basic approach. No doubt the difference is linked above all to the fact that the original bases were in one case empiricism and in the other speculative idealism. I remember very well that, in the letter that he wrote to me at the time of the publication of *Être et Avoir*, Bergson expressed to me the impossibility in which he found himself of *situating* my thought with regard to his own. This impossibility was linked, I am convinced, to the fact that the starting points [*références originelles*] were themselves irreducible to each other. And yet in [without?] the Bergsonian venture and the admirable courage it gave proof of, it is probable that I would never have had either the valor or even simply the ability to take up my own research. The more I apply myself to discerning its nature—and I am not unaware how appropriate it is to mistrust *a posteriori* reconstructions—the more *the hegemony of music* in this development appears to me incontestable. And I suppose that in works such as *Pelléas* and *Ariane* there is established between the musical universe and the other universes a contact that, for me, was in some degree lacking in the great classical or even romantic works with which I had nourished myself up until then. To be sure, the word 'contact' here is very inadequate. But what I mean is that the notion of a musical truth allowed itself here, in spite of everything, to be more directly approached, a truth conceived of as a fidelity. "Fidelity to what?" you will ask. All the mystery resides precisely in this double fact that, on the one hand, we have the invincible assurance that this word 'fidelity' has a meaning as precise in music as in the world of spiritual relations, but that, on the other hand, we surely do not have direct access to an object-reality (*réalité-objet*) with relation to which this fidelity could be defined.

Perhaps I will make myself a little better understood if I say this it is this fidelity that is itself the only way of access. But this surely does not signify, as some philosophers of the past would have wanted us to believe, that this fidelity in some way engenders its object. And here another category comes into play whose importance music alone revealed to me at the outset, and this is the category of humility. It is scarcely necessary to say that the Moussorgsky of *Boris* and the art-songs was for me at the origin of this discovery and that this revelation took place in opposition to the exaltation unleashed by Wagner's hubris (which does not mean, however, that I have ever rejected either *Tristan* or *Die Meistersänger* or the *Ring Cycle*—excommunications of this sort seem to me even today absurd and scandalous.) If then I am not mistaken in this difficult and risky reconstruction, I would have reason to think that these categories (whose metaphysical meaning I have attempted to specify, particularly beginning with 1930) had been in a way presented to me most concretely in the great lyric works I have mentioned.

The special function of *Ariane et Barbe-Bleu* in this development was probably a little different. I have previously attempted to specify it in a note that I sent to Paul Dukas, of which, I think, he was essentially quite willing to approve. In *Ariane*, beyond the admirable Andante of the *Sonata* and the most beautiful of the *Variations*, I thought I saw a certain tragic wisdom revealing itself to me, a wisdom entirely in harmony with what was then the deepest exigency of my being. And to tell the truth, I am inclined to think that this need is more than moderately important. I recognize this exigency in myself today just as deep as it ever was, even if it has some difficulty in harmonizing with other no less fundamental needs that are themselves authentically Christian. I no longer know precisely who at the time brought out the basically Nietzschean character of that tragic wisdom that was expressed in the last scene of *Ariane*—this scene that inwardly overwhelmed my friends and me. And when I think of my friend, I am thinking especially of the genius Henri Franck, the author of the *Danse devant l'Arche*, who succumbed in 1912 to the same disease of which his similarly gifted uncle died at the same age. Need I say that this Nietzscheanism was entirely purified, that indeed it had nothing to do with the immoralism of Gide? It was Franck who, before his conversion, was to exercise so lasting an effect on Charles Du Bos—the Nietzscheanism of inward probity and also of the *schenkende Tugend* [gift-giving virtue]. Will someone say that I am illegitimately substituting here Maeterlinck's poem for the music of Dukas? But here more than anywhere else, the encounter takes on an ontological meaning. The *Ariane* of Maeterlinck appears as preordained to the *Ariane* of Dukas, which is itself the unique, exemplary incarnation of a musical thought.

Moreover, one must not believe that this profound meaning of the work was universally understood at that time. I remember very well the exasperation we felt, Henry Franck and I, when Jacques Riviere devoted to *Nouvelle Revue Francaise* a note on the lyrical drama of Dukas in which almost all he praised was the revolt of the peasants, that is, what was most exterior in the work. Jacques Riviere, who had so passionately loved and understood *Pelléas* and also *Boris* [*Goudanov* by Moussorgsky], I think, and who a little later was to be one of the first to greet the *Sacre du Printemps* [of Stravinsky], *remained* completely uncomprehending of Dukas' world, which was on the contrary so intimately our own. (It is once again the memory of Henri Franck that I associate here with my own meditation.) The letters published in the *Cahiers Verts* make this perfectly clear. I think in particular of the one in which he said to me (in Sept. 1910) "if thought is identical to being, one must add that thought 'in itself,' defined with regard to what is most essential to it, is not knowledge." This assertion to which, at the outset, I doubtless would not have subscribed without some hesitation, corresponded nonetheless to my deepest conviction, a conviction that was to take form subsequently, always in the light of music. And I will not hesitate today to declare that, if I have little by little turned away from the theory of knowledge, it is precisely because I have become ever more aware of this transcendence of thought with regard to the use it makes of itself when it applies itself to objects and to the relationships that link them together. It is without any doubt in the last works of Beethoven, or more exactly through them, that I became most clearly aware of this higher destination of thought. But amongst our contemporaries Dukas is no doubt the one who seemed to me to participate the most directly in this sublime heritage.

Subsequently, it undoubtedly Gabriel Fauré who, after Debussy and Dukas, was to command most fully my admiration. And the word 'admiration' is still too cold and too distant. Curiously, it was the final works of Fauré that won me over forever, and it is starting from them that I made my way back to the preceding works whose seemingly facile character had decidedly turned we away in the beginning. The prodigious importance of Fauré's major works—and I am thinking both of the chamber music works beginning with the first quintet and of the songs beginning with the *Chanson d'Eve*—consists perhaps essentially for me in that one sees there the most *improbable* union of pure thought and *essential* sensibility. Here again I think I see the starting point of an entirely renewed philosophical reflection. For this music, so distilled that, in a certain way, it is nothing but form, is yet, on reflection, as freed as is possible from any formal element, if this word is taken in its usual essentially academic and scholastic meaning. Form here becomes a being just as it happens with the greatest masters of drawing, the ones who are the most freed from all the traditions of the school. But at the same time the most mysterious synthesis seems to take place here between pure form and pure emotion. And the very fact that this synthesis is possible, that it is obvious, leads us to ask ourselves about the nature of emotion, and no doubt to go beyond all the attempts at explanation that have been proposed by current psychology.

I must content myself here with these indications that may seem hermetic to more than one reader and that cannot in fact take shape in formulas satisfying for the mind and easily transmissible. For they are in my eyes above all a value of transcendence and of propulsion. They contribute perhaps to making possible this setting loose of thought that is the primordial condition of any metaphysics worthy of the name.

Beginning with these notes we would eventually meet up with certain of the categories, themselves mysterious, that contemporary German poetry and philosophy have introduced (I am thinking of Rilke and Heidegger) and with which commentators are still battling rather painfully. I have in mind both [Heidegger's notion of] the *Open* and [Rilke's] *interior cosmic space* (*Weltinnenraum*). If I have any deep-rooted conviction it is that at the point we have reached philosophical thought can no longer, without being in danger of losing all its effectiveness, be dissociated from a reflection on the work of art. What is more, the work should be no longer considered as a thing or an object but according to its process of elaboration and also according to its function, or rather let us say its destination in a spiritual economy. Moreover, such an economy in its almost unfathomable complexity is, more and more difficult to control or interpret. But precisely the work of art—and as for me I am thinking most especially of the *melos*—exists to give us an immediate access to a simplicity that is beyond this very complexity.

It is in this perspective that I cannot omit considering the place that my ephemeral musical creation of the years 1946-47 has occupied in my work. No doubt it was necessary that it should be given to me to be, at least for a little while, no longer simply a listener or contemplator, but to participate directly in this musical *Being* whose dignity has always been sovereign for me. These songs that were awakened in me by contact with admired poems—whether by Valéry, Supervielle, Rilke, Hoffmansthal, or many others still—that present themselves to me as the most concrete witness possible of this absolute experience, one that is not subjective but *intersubjective*, that I have tried not to define but to approach or evoke in my recent philosophical writings. Of these songs I could never say that they come *from me* in any sense. And perhaps it is no more reasonable to say that they came *from elsewhere*. Fundamentally they are situated precisely in a zone where this distinction, this contrast, loses all meaning. And here too it is the unfortunately hackneyed expression of transcendence that presents itself to my mind. That I was able to experience thus directly and concretely the categories that many years earlier, during an inquiry that was groping but perhaps undertaken with music as a starting point, I had attempted to define in rigorously abstract terms. This is something for which I will never be too sufficiently grateful to the powers that in some manner are in charge of the destiny of our lives and our work. I would simply wish that the kind of thanksgiving with which I would like to end this meditation should be interpreted as the act of humility to which we must be led, I think, by any reflection on what we are and the insignificance of what we *can* do by ourselves, on the infinite dependence wherein we must recognize our only valid reasons for belief and hope.

Note

[1] This article appeared originally in *La Revue musicale*, n. 210, January, 1952.

The Irruption of Melody

For many years I have found in improvisation more than just a refuge. It was an incomparable mode of interior self-repossession. And even this does not say enough. It was not just the means for reassembling these parcels of the soul that life constrains us to disperse into distinct tasks, into occupations without conclusion in which sometimes a pathway seemed to be starting but was subsequently lost in fatigue among repetitions, leaving us dissatisfied, confusedly anxious. While it is true that for me improvisation has functioned perfectly as a way of recollecting myself, it is has done so only by bringing about this link between myself and myself that daily life constantly breaks, and, much more intimately still, and by means of a grace of which I cannot give an account, by restoring to me through the sacrament of sound all those who have shared in my life. No doubt this experience and that of *Time Regained* in Proust correspond in some fashion. And yet I think I perceive notable differences between them. It is not a matter here of recreating a past experienced anew in its freshness and, as it were, free from all the grime with which a utilitarian memory coats it. No: what is here in question is much rather a sublimation that tends to convert into essences the beings that it has been given to me either to cherish or simply to envelop with a glance of momentary longing... It is as if, in musical improvisation, this longing—a longing to which so often the mutual knowing of erotic love [*co-naissance érotique*] can contribute only the most precarious and the most fallacious satisfactions—found a marvelous though fleeting answer to a prayer. "Although fleeting," did I say? Everything seems to happen as though, thanks to these momentary encounters, impossible to renew, impossible to describe or evoke, that there takes place this consolidation [*remembrement*] of everything that, through the evil conspirings of cautiousness and chance, has in the course of our lives been wasted, scattered, and, to judge only by the appearances, lost forever.

To be sure, this joy of improvisation, in a way a sacred joy, was accompanied for me by a poignant regret. How many times has my heart not been stricken by the thought that, beginning in adolescence, I ought to have studied music intensively and then devoted myself to composition. It seemed to me that it was at the same time an irrevocably lost opportunity. It took some chance circumstances, the details of which scarcely matter, that were required for me to resolve to translate musically certain of my favorite poems. I should have liked to be able to describe here the way in which the relationship between poem and music imposed itself on me. What I was able to notice each time was that, to the precise degree that the poem had authority over me, or that I had submitted myself to its dominating presence, I felt a musical thought flowing towards me that at first took me by surprise but in which subsequently I saw myself most clearly. For me at least the poem could not be reduced to a simple pretext taken over by a whim whose primary concern was to give itself free reign. In this matter I have been able to verify everything Paul Valéry has declared regarding the stimulating and propulsive value of constraints. These constraints, moreover, are linked to the presence, at the very source of the poem, of a being who not only composes it but who sings it and who is, above all, a voice. How one would like to be able to have recourse here, as in other languages, to those reflexive verbal phrases that translate so perfectly the incantatory act: *sich hinein singen, to sing oneself into....* I think I have noted elsewhere that the intonation is here a mediator between the poem and the music. It is thus that, attempting to write an art song for *Le Vin perdu* of Paul Valéry, I found my leverage in the interrogative accent that gives to this short piece its emotional value: "Who desired your loss, O nectar?" The musical phrase imposed itself upon me with an irresistible proof. And it is around this descent, this gliding toward an unformulable secret that all the rest of the song organized itself. But inversely, poems that I admire, certain poems of Henri de Regnier for example, that seemed to exclude any possibility of intonation, have revealed themselves to me as musically intransposable. No doubt one would need to add further nuances here. Intonation that can serve as a support for musical creation seems to me in a general way irreducible to oratorical intonation of any kind. It is indissolubly linked to the values of intimacy, with the latter not excluding, moreover, any metaphysical *nisus*. But such values only exclude the search for the effect to be obtained, the attitude adopted to make an impression, to convince, intimidate or touch a listener on whose adhesion or submission one is counting. It is regrettable that the word *forain* [fair-ground] gives so little of the adjective *forensis* [Latin for 'forensic'] from which it is nonetheless derived, for the latter word seems to me to apply exactly to everything that is refractory to an authentic musical translation, at least in the register of the melody. One can thus see why a poet like Victor Hugo has almost never inspired musicians. Perhaps one would have to say in short that, from the moment when a word is used, where it becomes a means, it tends to separate itself from music. I agree, moreover, that one is here entering into a zone filled with subtleties. Does it not seem in fact at first blush that prayer or invocation, so manifestly permeable to musical inspiration, implies a use of the word? But would that not be to play with words? Prayer, whether or not expressed by words, because it aims at a response or the granting of a request that is not of a sensory order, if it is not itself silent, is at the very least indissolubly wed to silence. It is no doubt for that reason that it is music and also that any music in its profoundest depths is prayer.

Note
[1] This article appeared originally in 1953.

Humanism and Music[1]

I had already read and I have just listened to the remarkable lecture of Mr. Stobel with all the attention that it deserves. Dare I say that I fear I may be in disagreement with him on several important points?

I would like first of all to wonder in what sense one can speak of humanism with regard to a musician or a musical work. In an historical perspective, I think this question can have a relatively clear answer insofar as in music, humanistic music can be contrasted with sacred music. Composers such as Monteverdi or Purcell are the ones that come to my mind here in the first place. In *Orfeo* or the *Coronation of Poppea* as in *Dido and Aeneas* we see purely human feeling accede to the superior dignity that the highest musical expression enables them to find. If, as is no doubt necessary, we have recourse to the language of the philosophy of values, we would have to say that the purely human values or the values that, at the very least, are not related to what I would call the "religious constellation," are here directly govern the inspiration of the musician. Lulli, Rameau, even Gluck are very certainly situated in the tradition of a musical humanism thus defined. On the other hand, I will say even now (and I will return to this point presently) that a Stravinsky who has explicitly declared that musical art should not express any feeling is thereby situated precisely outside of any humanism.

To be sure, where it is applied to music, the word 'express' is subject to reservation; and it would certainly be better to try to avoid it, even when one is speaking of the musicians I have named. Whenever I have reflected on this difficult and fascinating problem, I have always thought that the verb 'express' or the verb 'transcribe' [*traduire*] cannot be rigorously applied to the intimate and original relation between music and feeling. It would seem to me much more precise to say that a true melody—that melody, the secret of which Stravinsky lost so early and forever—an authentic melody, I say, is feeling itself, beginning from the point when it has undergone the transmutation that enables it to become form or essence in place of being simply undergone or experienced. By all indications one misunderstands the deep and mysterious nature of this transmutation, or perhaps simply its autonomous quality, when one imagines, in very puerile fashion, that the musician tries to transcribe a given feeling by means of sounds. The truth is much rather that this feeling is not given to him as such. Quite possibly he can even be unaware of it. He is the *place* where the transmutation takes place. And this is the reason why it is so profoundly absurd to ask a composer what he means to express in his quartet or his symphony. Nonetheless, feeling is or must be at the very beginning of musical creation; and it is to be expected, it is even no doubt necessary, that the hearing of the completed musical work frees in us this feeling that has given birth to the work, moreover, without our being able most of the time to specify it in any way.

I will say, on the other hand, that humanism in a Mozart or especially in a Beethoven takes on characteristics noticeably different from those that it may have had in their predecessors. Beethoven's last works are, in all likelihood, the highest expression ever attained by humanism in music. One can say that it is an heroic humanism we are dealing with here, but one in which the humanism never ceases to interiorize itself, divesting itself from the rhetorical or, if you wish, the theatrical element it may have had at the outset. The last sonatas, the last quartets accomplish on the level of musical creation, in a sovereign way, the conquest that will be attempted in quite a different sphere and in always precarious conditions by Nietzsche or by the philosophies of existence. One is rather tempted to say that, whereas the humanism of the musicians of the seventeenth or eighteenth centuries remained, in spite of everything, in a way turned towards the past and appears as it were illumined by the last rays of Greek thought, Beethoven's humanism in contrast is turned towards the future or perhaps more essentially towards a rediscovered eternity of which what we call the future is after all only an illusory and in a way mythical expression.

But in such a perspective where will we find anything in our contemporaries that can be described as humanism? Certainly not, I will answer, in Debussy: his genius in any case is not in question, for we see in him, in contrast, a man allowing himself to be, as it were, invested and at last penetrated by the mysterious powers of nature. Everything occurs as if the man were the site of a mysterious burgeoning that tends to cover over, I would say almost to bury him and the extraordinary and mysterious sadness of this art is that of a death-agony, as it happens much more sensuous than tragic. The great humanist of French music is Fauré whom I place, for my part, among the greatest. From the very first art-songs, from the very first violin sonata up to the final works, whether we are talking about *Prométhée* or *Pénélope* or especially the major works of chamber music, the two *Quintets*, the second *Violin Sonata* or the second *Cello Concerto* and, of course, the *String Quartet*, we witness the ascension of a soul who, freeing himself from the traps of the sentimentalism in which it could have been caught at the beginning, accedes little by little to the noblest and most purified expression of a sensibility that altogether becomes form, becomes melody.

In Stravinsky we observe a very different and, as it were, opposite spectacle. To be sure, nothing could have surpassed the brilliance of his first works. But quite quickly, he suffered an inner sterilization of which perhaps only an authentic psychoanalysis, that is to say, one freed from Freudian tics, could reveal the secret to us. As a result, this musician, so prodigiously endowed at the outset, has come to substitute a work of pure formal invention for that inward conquest that, in the great musicians of the past without exception, never allows itself to be separated from the discovery of forms. I will not hesitate to say, as far as I am concerned, that Stravinsky seems to turn his back on the human. Of course, he may imagine that he is transcending it. There are, however, many—and I am one of them—who think, on the contrary, that this so-called transcendence is nothing but a regression.

In what concerns Schönberg and his school, particularly the Alban Berg of *Wozzeck*, I will no doubt be less definite, although I admit I am fairly skeptical about the truly humane value of the territories that this music has annexed to the world of auditory expression. As with Debussy, but in a completely different way, because it seems to me that the feeling for nature is here infinitely less rich and less lively, we are witnessing a dehumanization in and by music. Perhaps at least it can be considered—and this is perhaps its greatness—as the very song of dereliction.

Note

[1] This article orginally appeared in 1954.

Index